Saginaw, Michigan

Renee Browning

Contents

Articles

Overview of Michigan — 1
- Michigan — 1
- History of Michigan — 33
- Geography of Michigan — 40
- List of Michigan state parks — 47
- List of National Historic Landmarks in Michigan — 52

Overview of Saginaw — 61
- Saginaw, Michigan — 61
- Saginaw County, Michigan — 74
- Flint/Tri-Cities — 82

History of Saginaw — 88
- History of Saginaw, Michigan — 88

Things to See In and Around Saginaw — 94
- Temple Theatre (Saginaw, Michigan) — 94
- Castle Museum (Saginaw, Michigan) — 95
- Fashion Square Mall — 97

Attractions — 99
- Saginaw Trail — 99
- Saginaw River — 107
- Saginaw Bay — 108
- Lake Huron — 110
- Dow Event Center — 118

Saginaw Spirit	120
Saginaw Sting	127

Transportation **131**

MBS International Airport	131
Bishop International Airport	135
Interstate 75	139
M-47 (Michigan highway)	147

References

Article Sources and Contributors	150
Image Sources, Licenses and Contributors	151

Overview of Michigan

Michigan

State of Michigan	
 Flag	 Seal
Nickname(s): The Great Lakes State, The Wolverine State	
Motto(s): Si quaeris peninsulam amoenam circumspice (If you seek a pleasant peninsula, look about you)	
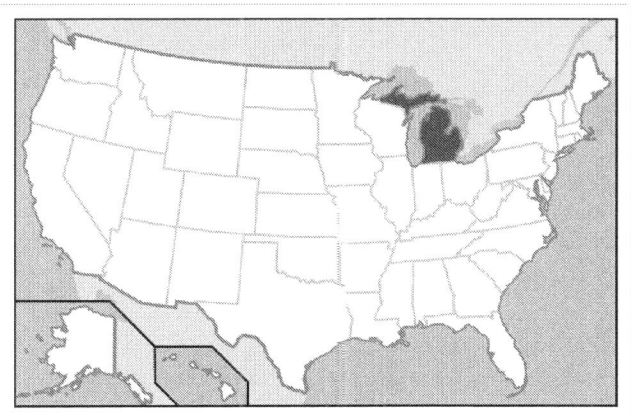	
Official language(s)	None (English, *de-facto*)
Demonym	Michigander Michiganian
Capital	Lansing
Largest city	Detroit
Largest metro area	Metro Detroit
Area	Ranked 11th in the US

- Total	97,990 sq mi (253,793 km^2)
- Width	386 miles (621 km)
- Length	456 miles (734 km)
- % water	41.5
- Latitude	41° 41' N to 48° 18' N
- Longitude	82° 7' W to 90° 25' W
Population	Ranked 8th in the US
- Total	10,045,697 (2008 est.)
- Density	179/sq mi (67.55/km^2) Ranked 16th in the US
- Median income	$44,627 (21st)
Elevation	
- Highest point	Mount Arvon 1,979 ft (603 m)
- Mean	902 ft (275 m)
- Lowest point	Lake Erie 571 ft (174 m)
Admission to Union	January 26, 1837 (26th)
Governor	Jennifer Granholm (D)
Lieutenant Governor	John D. Cherry (D)
Legislature	Michigan Legislature
- Upper house	Senate
- Lower house	House of Representatives
U.S. Senators	• Carl Levin (D) • Debbie Stabenow (D)
U.S. House delegation	8 Democrats 7 Republicans (list)
Time zones	
- most of state	Eastern: UTC-5/-4
- 4 U.P. counties	Central: UTC-6/-5

Abbreviations	MI Mich. US-MI
Website	http://www.michigan.gov

Michigan (ⁱ /ˈmɪʃɪɡən/) is a U.S. state located in the Great Lakes Region of the United States of America. The name Michigan is a French corruption of the Ojibwe word *mishigama*, meaning "large water" or "large lake".

Michigan is the eighth most populous state in the United States. It has the longest freshwater shoreline of any political subdivision in the world, being bounded by four of the five Great Lakes, plus Lake Saint Clair. In 2005, Michigan ranked third among US states for the number of registered recreational boats, behind California and Florida. Michigan has 64,980 inland lakes and ponds. A person in the state is never more than six miles (10 km) from a natural water source or more than 87.2 miles (140.3 km) from a Great Lakes shoreline. It is the largest state by total area east of the Mississippi River.

Michigan is the only state to consist entirely of two peninsulas. The Lower Peninsula, to which the name Michigan was originally applied, is often dubbed "the mitten" by residents, owing to its shape. The Upper Peninsula (often referred to as "The U.P.") is separated from the Lower Peninsula by the Straits of Mackinac, a five-mile (8 km)-wide channel that joins Lake Huron to Lake Michigan. The Upper Peninsula is economically important for tourism and natural resources.

History

See also: Timeline of Michigan history, History of railroads in Michigan, History of Michigan, and History of Detroit

Michigan was home to Native American cultures before colonization by Europeans. When the first European explorers arrived, the most populous and influential tribes were Algonquian peoples, specifically, the *Ottawa*, the *Anishnabe* (called *Chippewa* in French, after their language *Ojibwe*), and the *Potawatomi*. The Anishnabe, whose numbers are estimated to have been between 25,000 and 35,000, were the most populous.

Although the Anishnabe were well-established in Michigan's Upper Peninsula and northern Lower Peninsula, they also inhabited northern Ontario, northern Wisconsin, southern Manitoba, and northern and north-central Minnesota. The Ottawa lived primarily south of the Straits of Mackinac in northern and western Michigan, while the Potawatomi were primarily in the southwest. The three nations co-existed peacefully as part of a loose confederation called the Council of Three Fires. Other First Nations people in Michigan, in the south and east, were the *Mascouten*, the *Menominee*, the *Miami*, and the Wyandot, who are better known by their French name, *Huron*.

17th century

French *voyageurs*, explored and settled in Michigan in the 17th century. The first Europeans to reach what later became Michigan were those of Étienne Brûlé's expedition in 1622. The first permanent European settlement was founded in 1668 on the site where Father (*Père*, in French) Jacques Marquette established Sault Ste. Marie, Michigan as a Catholic mission to minister to the Ottawa Indians, and to serve as a regional headquarters for further Catholic missionary activities in the upper Great Lakes area. It was here that the first European building was erected in Michigan, within the US Midwest, and also within what is now the Canadian province of Ontario.

Soon afterward, in 1671 the outlying mission of Saint Ignace was founded approximately 50 miles (80 km) south. Then in 1675, French Catholic missionaries founded Marquette approximately 200 miles (320 km) to the west of Sault Ste. Marie, on the south shore of Lake Superior. Together with Sault Ste. Marie, these three original Jesuit missions are the first three European-founded cities in Michigan. Jesuit missionaries were well received by the Indian populations in the area, with relatively few difficulties or hostilities. "The Soo" (Sault Ste. Marie) has the distinction of being the oldest city in both Michigan and Ontario. It was split into two cities in 1818, a year after the U.S.-Canada boundary in the Great Lakes was finally established by the U.S.-U.K. Joint Border Commission following the War of 1812.

In 1679, Lord La Salle of France directed the construction of the *Griffin*, the first European sailing vessel built on the upper Great Lakes. That same year, La Salle built Fort Miami at present-day St. Joseph.

18th century

In 1701, French explorer and army officer Antoine de la Mothe Cadillac founded Le Fort Ponchartrain du Détroit or "Fort Ponchartrain on-the-Strait" on the strait, known as the Detroit River, between lakes Saint Clair and Erie. Cadillac had convinced King Louis XIV's chief minister, Louis Phélypeaux, Comte de Pontchartrain, that a permanent community there would strengthen French control over the upper Great Lakes and repel British aspirations. Cadillac served as the French governor of Louisiana from 1710 to 1716.

Michigan in 1718, Guillaume de L'Isle map, approximate state area highlighted.

The hundred soldiers and workers who accompanied Cadillac built a fort enclosing one arpent (about 0.85 acres (3400 m^2), the equivalent of just under 200 feet (61 m) per side) and named it Fort Pontchartrain. Cadillac's wife, Marie Thérèse Guyon, soon moved to Detroit, becoming one of the first European women to settle in the Michigan wilderness. The town quickly became a major fur-trading and shipping post. The *Église de Saint-Anne* (Church of Saint Ann) was founded the same year. While the original building does not survive, the congregation of that name continues to be active today.

At the same time, the French strengthened Fort Michilimackinac at the Straits of Mackinac to better control their lucrative fur-trading empire. By the mid-18th century, the French also occupied forts at present-day Niles and Sault Ste. Marie, though most of the rest of the region remained unsettled by Europeans.

From 1660 to the end of French rule, Michigan was part of the Royal Province of New France. In 1759, following the Battle of the Plains of Abraham in the French and Indian War (1754–1763), Québec City fell to British forces. This marked Britain's victory in the Seven Years War. Under the 1763 Treaty of Paris, Michigan and the rest of New France east of the Mississippi River passed to Great Britain.

During the American Revolutionary War, Detroit was an important British supply center. Most of the inhabitants were French-Canadians or Native Americans, many of whom had been allied with the French. Because of imprecise cartography and unclear language defining the boundaries in the 1763 Treaty of Paris, the British retained control of Detroit and Michigan after the American Revolution. When Quebec split into Lower and Upper Canada in 1790, Michigan was part of Kent County, Upper Canada. It held its first democratic elections in August 1792 to send delegates to the new provincial parliament at Newark (now Niagara-on-the-Lake).

Under terms negotiated in the 1794 Jay Treaty, Britain withdrew from Detroit and Michilimackinac in 1796. Questions remained over the boundary for many years, and the United States did not have uncontested control of the Upper Peninsula and Drummond Island until 1818 and 1847, respectively.

19th century

During the War of 1812, Michigan Territory (effectively consisting of Detroit and the surrounding area) was captured by the British and nominally returned to Upper Canada. United States forces pushed the British out in 1813 and moved into Canada.

The Treaty of Ghent implemented the policy of *Status Quo Ante Bellum* or "Just as Things Were Before the War." That meant Michigan would remain as part of the United States, and the agreement to establish a joint US-UK boundary commission also remained valid. Subsequent to the findings of that commission in 1817, control of the Upper Peninsula and of islands in the St. Clair River delta was transferred from Ontario to Michigan in 1818. Mackinac Island (to which the British had moved their Michilimackinac army base) was transferred to the U.S. in 1847.

The population grew slowly until the opening of the Erie Canal in New York State 1825 brought a large influx of settlers. Commodities such as grain, lumber, and iron ore could be shipped via the Great Lakes through the Erie Canal and Hudson River. By the 1830s, Michigan had 80,000 residents. More than enough to apply and qualify for statehood. The waterway connection among the Great Lakes states increased the wealth of all.

In October 1835 the people approved the Constitution of 1835, thereby forming a state government, although Congressional recognition was delayed pending resolution of a boundary dispute with Ohio. Both states claimed a 468-square-mile (1,210 km^2) strip of land that included the newly incorporated city of Toledo on Lake Erie and an

Lumbering pines in the late 1800s

area to the west then known as the "Great Black Swamp". The dispute came to be called the Toledo War. Michigan and Ohio militia maneuvered in the area but never exchanged fire. Congress awarded the "Toledo Strip" to Ohio. Michigan received the western part of the Upper Peninsula as a concession and formally entered the Union on January 26, 1837.

The Upper Peninsula proved to be a rich source of lumber, iron, and copper. These were among the state's most sought-after natural resources. Geologist Douglass Houghton and land surveyor William Austin Burt were among the first to document many of these resources. Developers rushed to the state. Michigan led the nation in lumber production from 1850s to the 1880s.

The first official meeting of the Republican Party took place July 6, 1854 in Jackson, Michigan, where the party adopted its platform. Michigan made a significant contribution to the Union in the American Civil War and sent more than forty regiments of volunteers to the Federal armies.

Communities and the state rapidly set up systems for public education, including founding the University of Michigan, for a classical academic education, and Ypsilanti Normal College (now Eastern Michigan University, for the training of teachers. Michigan State University in East Lansing was founded as a land-grant college. In the early 20th century, Michigan was the first state to offer a four-year curriculum in a normal college.

20th century to present

See also: History of Ford Motor Company

Michigan's economy underwent a transformation at the turn of the 20th century. The birth of the automotive industry, with Henry Ford's first plant in Highland Park, marked the beginning of a new era in transportation. Like the steamship and railroad, it was a far-reaching development. More than the forms of public transportation, the automobile transformed private life. It became the major industry of Detroit and Michigan, and permanently altered the socio-economic life of the United States and much of the world.

With the growth, the auto industry created jobs in Detroit that attracted immigrants from Europe and migrants from across the country, including both whites and blacks from the rural South. By 1910 Detroit was the fourth largest city in the nation. Residential housing was in short supply, and it took years for the market to catch up with the population boom. By the 1930s, so many immigrants had arrived that more than 30 languages were spoken in the public schools, and ethnic communities celebrated in annual heritage festivals.

Many African Americans moved to Detroit as one of the destinations in the Great Migration from the South, as they could find better work there. Over the years they contributed greatly to its diverse urban culture. African Americans from Detroit created national popular music trends, such as the influential Motown Sound of the 1960s led by a variety of individual singers and groups.

Grand Rapids, the second-largest city in Michigan, is also an important center of manufacturing. Since 1838, the city had also been noted for its thriving furniture industry. Started because of ready sources of lumber, the furniture industry declined in the late 20th century through competition with other regional firms and overseas industry.

Michigan held its first United States presidential primary election in 1910. With its rapid growth in industry, it was an important center of union industry-wide organizing, such as the rise of the United Auto Workers.

In 1920 WWJ in Detroit became the first radio station in the United States to regularly broadcast commercial programs. Throughout that decade, some of the country's largest and most ornate skyscrapers were built in the city. Particularly noteworthy are the Fisher Building, Cadillac Place, and the Guardian Building, each of which is a National Historic Landmarks (NHL).

Detroit boomed through the 1950s, at one point doubling its population in a decade. After World War II, housing development grew outside cities. Newly built highways allowed commuters to navigate the region more easily. In Detroit as elsewhere, many began to move to newer housing in the suburbs.

Michigan is the leading auto-producing state in the U.S., although some of the industry has shifted to less-expensive labor in the Southern United States and overseas. With more than ten million residents, Michigan remains a large and influential state, ranking eighth in population among the fifty states.

The Metro Detroit area in the southeast corner of the state is the largest metropolitan area in Michigan (roughly 50% of the population resides there) and one of the ten largest metropolitan areas in the country. The Grand Rapids/Holland/Muskegon metropolitan area on the west side of the state is the fastest-growing metro area in the state, with over 1.3 million residents as of 2006.

Metro Detroit's population is growing. Detroit's population is stabilizing with a strong redevelopment in the city's central district with a significant rise in population in its outskirts are contributing to some population inflow. A period of economic transition, especially in manufacturing, has caused economic difficulties in the region since the recession of 2001.

Government

See also: List of Governors of Michigan and United States congressional delegations from Michigan

State government

Main article: Government of Michigan

Michigan is governed as a republic, with three branches of government: the executive branch consisting of the Governor of Michigan and the other independently elected constitutional officers; the legislative branch consisting of the House of Representatives and Senate; and the judicial branch consisting of the one court of justice. The state also allows direct participation of the electorate by initiative, referendum, recall, and ratification. Lansing is the state capital and is home to all three branches of state government.

The Governor of Michigan and the other state constitutional officers serve four-year terms and may be re-elected only once. The current Governor is Jennifer Granholm. Michigan has two official Governor's Residences; one is in Lansing, and the other is at Mackinac Island.

The Michigan Legislature consists of a 38-member Senate and 110-member House of Representatives. Senators serve four-year terms and Representatives two. The Michigan State Capitol was dedicated in 1879 and has hosted the state's executive and legislative branches ever since.

Law

The Michigan Court System consists of two courts with primary jurisdiction (the Circuit Courts and the District Courts), one intermediate level appellate court (the Michigan Court of Appeals), and the Michigan Supreme Court. There are several administrative courts and specialized courts. The Michigan Constitution provides for voter initiative and referendum (Article II, § 9, defined as "the power to propose laws and to enact and reject laws, called the initiative, and the power to approve or reject laws enacted by the legislature, called the referendum. The power of initiative extends only to laws which the legislature may enact under this constitution").

In 1846 Michigan was the first state in the Union, as well as the first English-speaking government in the world, to abolish the death penalty. Historian David Chardavoyne has suggested that the movement to abolish capital punishment in Michigan grew as a result of enmity toward the state's neighbor, Canada. Under British rule, it made public executions a regular practice.

Politics

See also: Elections in Michigan and Political party strength in Michigan

Michigan Governor Jennifer Granholm (D)

Presidential elections results

Year	Republicans	Democrats
2008	40.89% 2,048,639	**57.33%** 2,872,579
2004	47.81% 2,313,746	**51.23%** 2,479,183
2000	46.14% 1,953,139	**51.28%** 2,170,418
1996	38.48% 1,481,212	**51.69%** 1,989,653
1992	36.38% 1,554,940	**43.77%** 1,871,182
1988	**53.57%** 1,965,486	45.67% 1,675,783
1984	**59.23%** 2,251,571	40.24% 1,529,638
1980	**48.99%** 1,915,225	42.50% 1,661,532
1976	**51.83%** 1,893,742	46.44% 1,696,714
1972	**56.20%** 1,961,721	41.81% 1,459,435
1968	41.46% 1,370,665	**48.18%** 1,593,082
1964	33.10% 1,060,152	**66.70%** 2,136,615
1960	48.84% 1,620,428	**50.85%** 1,687,269

Voters in the state elect candidates from both major parties. Economic issues are important in Michigan elections. The three-term Republican Governor John Engler (1991–2003) preceded the current

Democratic Governor Jennifer Granholm. The state has re-elected its current Republican Attorney General Mike Cox since 2003. Michigan supported the election of Republican Presidents Ronald Reagan and George H.W. Bush.

However, the state has supported Democrats in the last five presidential election cycles. In 2008, Barack Obama carried the state over John McCain, winning Michigan's seventeen electoral votes with 57% of the vote. Democrats have won each of the last three, nine of the last ten, and fifteen of the last eighteen U.S. Senate elections in Michigan with confidence on national economic issues posing a challenge. Republican strength is greatest in the western, northern, and rural parts of the state, especially in the Grand Rapids area. Republicans also do well in suburban Detroit, which tends to be an important factor in deciding statewide elections. Democrats are strongest in the east, especially in the cities of Detroit, Ann Arbor, Flint, and Saginaw.

Historically, the first formal meeting of the Republican Party took place in Jackson, Michigan on July 6, 1854 and the party thereafter dominated Michigan until the Great Depression. In the 1912 election, Michigan was one of the six states to support progressive Republican and third-party candidate Theodore Roosevelt for President after he lost the Republican nomination to William Howard Taft.

Michigan remained fairly reliably Republican at the presidential level for much of the 20th century. It was part of Greater New England, the northern tier of states settled chiefly by migrants from New England who carried their culture with them. The state was one of only a handful to back Wendell Willkie over Franklin Roosevelt in 1940, and supported Thomas E. Dewey in his losing bid against Harry Truman in 1948. Michigan went to the Democrats in presidential elections during the 1960s, and voted for Republican Richard Nixon in 1972.

Michigan was the home of Gerald Ford, the 38th President of the United States. He was born in Nebraska and moved as an infant to Grand Rapids, Michigan, and grew up there. The Gerald R. Ford Museum is located in Grand Rapids.

Administrative divisions

Main article: Administrative divisions of Michigan

See also: List of Michigan county seats, List of counties in Michigan, and List of municipalities in Michigan (by population)

State government is decentralized among three tiers — statewide, county and township. Counties are administrative divisions of the state, and townships are administrative divisions of a county. Both of them exercise state government authority, localized to meet the particular needs of their jurisdictions, as provided by state law. There are 83 counties in Michigan.

Cities, state universities, and villages are vested with home rule powers of varying degrees. Home rule cities can generally do anything that is not prohibited by law. The fifteen state universities have broad power and can do anything within the parameters of their status as educational institutions that is not prohibited by the state constitution. Villages, by contrast, have limited home rule and are not completely autonomous from the county and township in which they are located.

There are two types of township in Michigan: *general law* township and *charter*. Charter township status was created by the Legislature in 1947 and grants additional powers and stream-lined administration in order to provide greater protection against annexation by a city. As of April 2001, there were 127 charter townships in Michigan. In general, charter townships have many of the same powers as a city but without the same level of obligations. For example, a charter township can have its own fire department, water and sewer department, police department, and so on—just like a city—but it is not *required* to have those things, whereas cities *must* provide those services. Charter townships can opt to use county-wide services instead, such as deputies from the county sheriff's office instead of a home-based force of ordinance officers.

Geography

Further information: Geography of Michigan, Protected areas of Michigan, and List of Michigan state parks

Michigan consists of two peninsulas that lie between 82°30' to about 90°30' west longitude, and are separated by the Straits of Mackinac. The 45th parallel north runs through the state—marked by highway signs and the Polar-Equator Trail—along a line including Mission Point Light near Traverse City, the towns of Gaylord and Alpena and Menominee in the Upper Peninsula. With the exception of two small areas that are drained by the Mississippi River by way of the Wisconsin River in the Upper Peninsula and by way of the Kankakee-Illinois River in the Lower Peninsula, Michigan is drained by the Great Lakes-St. Lawrence watershed and is the only state with the majority of its land thus drained.

The Great Lakes that border Michigan from east to west are Lake Erie, Lake Huron, Lake Michigan and Lake Superior. It has more lighthouses than any other state. The state is bounded on the south by the states of Ohio and Indiana, sharing land and water boundaries with both. Michigan's western boundaries are almost entirely water boundaries, from south to north, with Illinois and Wisconsin in Lake Michigan; then a land boundary with Wisconsin and the Upper Peninsula, that is principally demarcated by the Menominee and Montreal Rivers; then water boundaries again, in Lake Superior, with Wisconsin and Minnesota to the west, capped around by the Canadian province of Ontario to the north and east.

Aerial view of Sleeping Bear Dunes.

Tahquamenon Falls in the Upper Peninsula of Michigan

The heavily forested Upper Peninsula is relatively mountainous in the west. The Porcupine Mountains, which are part of one of the oldest mountain chains in the world, rise to an altitude of almost 2,000 feet (610 m) above sea level and form the watershed between the streams flowing into Lake Superior and Lake Michigan. The surface on either side of this range is rugged. The state's highest point, in the Huron Mountains northwest of Marquette, is Mount Arvon at 1979 feet (603 m). The peninsula is as large as Connecticut, Delaware, Massachusetts, and Rhode Island combined but has fewer than 330,000 inhabitants. They are sometimes called "Yoopers" (from "U.P.'ers"), and their speech (the "Yooper dialect") has been heavily influenced by the numerous Scandinavian and Canadian immigrants who settled the area during the lumbering and mining boom of the late 19th century.

The Lower Peninsula, shaped like a mitten, is 277 miles (446 km) long from north to south and 195 miles (314 km) from east to west and occupies nearly two-thirds of the state's land area. The surface of the peninsula is generally level, broken by conical hills and glacial moraines usually not more than a few hundred feet tall. It is divided by a low water divide running north and south. The larger portion of the state is on the west of this and gradually slopes toward Lake Michigan. The highest point in the Lower Peninsula is either Briar Hill at 1705 feet (520 m), or one of several points nearby in the vicinity of Cadillac. The lowest point is the surface of Lake Erie at 571 feet (174 m).

The Pointe Mouillee State Game Area

The geographic orientation of Michigan's peninsulas makes for a long distance between the ends of the state. Ironwood, in the far western Upper Peninsula, lies 630 highway miles (1,015 km) from Lambertville in the Lower Peninsula's southeastern corner. The geographic isolation of the Upper Peninsula from Michigan's political and population centers makes the U.P. culturally and economically distinct. Occasionally U.P. residents have called for secession from Michigan and establishment as a new state to be called "Superior".

A feature of Michigan that gives it the distinct shape of a mitten is the Thumb. This peninsula projects out into Lake Huron and the Saginaw Bay. The geography of the Thumb is mainly flat with a few rolling hills. Other peninsulas of Michigan include the Keweenaw Peninsula, making up the Copper Country region of the state. The Leelanau Peninsula lies in the Northern Lower Michigan region. *See Also Michigan Regions*

Little Sable Point Light south of Pentwater, Michigan.

Numerous lakes and marshes mark both peninsulas, and the coast is much indented. Keweenaw Bay, Whitefish Bay, and the Big and Little Bays De Noc are the principal indentations on the Upper Peninsula. The Grand and Little Traverse, Thunder, and Saginaw bays indent the Lower Peninsula. Michigan has the ninth longest shoreline of any state—3224 miles (5189 km), including 1056 miles (1699 km) of island shoreline.

The state has numerous large islands, the principal ones being the North Manitou and South Manitou, Beaver, and Fox groups in Lake Michigan; Isle Royale and Grande Isle in Lake Superior; Marquette, Bois Blanc, and Mackinac islands in Lake Huron; and Neebish, Sugar, and Drummond islands in St. Mary's River. Michigan has about 150 lighthouses, the most of any U.S. state. The first lighthouses in Michigan were built between 1818 and 1822. They were built to project light at night and to serve as a landmark during the day to safely guide the passenger ships and freighters traveling the Great Lakes. See Lighthouses in the United States.

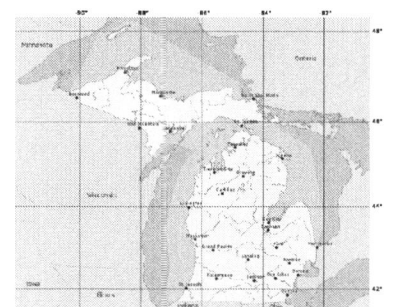
Michigan map, including territorial waters

The state's rivers are generally small, short and shallow, and few are navigable. The principal ones include the Detroit River, St. Marys River, and St. Clair River which connect the Great Lakes; the Au Sable, Cheboygan, and Saginaw, which flow into Lake Huron; the Ontonagon, and Tahquamenon, which flow into Lake Superior; and the St. Joseph, Kalamazoo, Grand, Muskegon, Manistee, and Escanaba, which flow into Lake Michigan. The state has 11,037 inland lakes and 38575 square miles (99910 km^2) of Great Lakes waters and rivers in addition to 1305 square miles (3380 km^2) of inland water. No point in Michigan is more than six miles (10 km) from an inland lake or more than 85 miles (137 km) from one of the Great Lakes.

The state is home to a number of areas maintained by the National Park Service including: Isle Royale National Park, located in Lake Superior, about 30 miles (48 km) southeast of Thunder Bay, Ontario. Other national protected areas in the state include: Keweenaw National Historical Park, Pictured Rocks National Lakeshore, Sleeping Bear Dunes National Lakeshore, Huron National Forest, Manistee National Forest, Hiawatha National Forest, Ottawa National Forest and Father Marquette National Memorial. The largest section of the North Country National Scenic Trail passes through Michigan.

Michigan

With 78 state parks, 19 state recreation areas, and 6 state forests, Michigan has the largest state park and state forest system of any state. These parks and forests include Holland State Park, Mackinac Island State Park, Au Sable State Forest, and Mackinaw State Forest.

Climate

Detroit, MI
Climate chart (explanation)
J F M A M J J A S O N D
average max. and min. temperatures in °F
precipitation totals in inches
source: Detroit Climate [1]

Metric conversion
J F M A M J J A S O N D
average max. and min. temperatures in °C
precipitation totals in mm

Lansing, MI
Climate chart (explanation)
J F M A M J J A S O N D
average max. and min. temperatures in °F
precipitation totals in inches
source: Lansing Climate [2]

Metric conversion
J F M A M J J A S O N D
average max. and min. temperatures in °C
precipitation totals in mm

Marquette, MI
Climate chart (explanation)
J | F | M | A | M | J | J | A | S | O | N | D
average max. and min. temperatures in °F
precipitation totals in inches
source: Marquette Climate [3]

Metric conversion
J | F | M | A | M | J | J | A | S | O | N | D
average max. and min. temperatures in °C
precipitation totals in mm

Michigan has a continental climate, although there are two distinct regions. The southern and central parts of the Lower Peninsula (south of Saginaw Bay and from the Grand Rapids area southward) have a warmer climate (Koppen climate classification *Dfa*) with hot summers and cold winters. The northern part of Lower Peninsula and the entire Upper Peninsula has a more severe climate (Koppen *Dfb*), with warm, but shorter summers and longer, cold to very cold winters. Some parts of the state average high temperatures below freezing from December through February, and into early March in the far northern parts. During the winter through the middle of February the state is frequently subjected to heavy lake-effect snow. The state averages from 30–40 inches (76–100 cm) of precipitation annually.

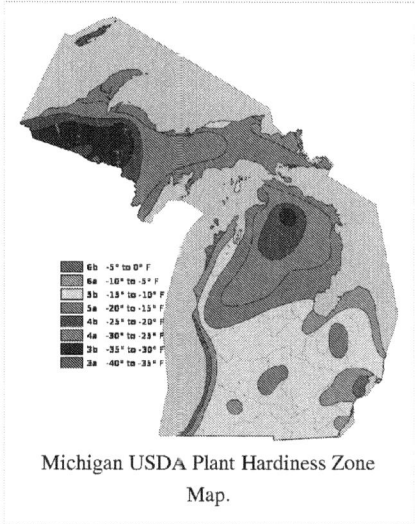

Michigan USDA Plant Hardiness Zone Map.

The entire state averages 30 days of thunderstorm activity per year. These can be severe, especially in the southern part of the state. The state averages 17 tornadoes per year, which are more common in the extreme southern portion of the state. Portions of the southern border have been nearly as vulnerable historically as parts of Tornado Alley. For this reason, many communities in the very southern portions of the state are equipped with tornado sirens to warn residents of approaching tornadoes. Farther north, in the Upper Peninsula, tornadoes are rare.

Monthly Normal High and Low Temperatures For Other Michigan Cities in °F(°C)												
City	Jan	Feb	Mar	Apr	May	Jun	Jul	Aug	Sep	Oct	Nov	Dec
Flint	29/13 (-2/-11)	32/15 (0/-9)	43/24 (6/-4)	56/35 (13/2)	69/45 (21/7)	78/55 (26/13)	82/59 (28/15)	80/57 (27/14)	72/49 (22/9)	60/39 (16/4)	46/30 (8/-1)	34/19 (1/-7)
Grand Rapids	29/16 (-2/-9)	33/17 (1/-8)	43/26 (6/-3)	57/36 (14/2)	70/47 (21/8)	78/56 (26/13)	82/60 (28/16)	80/59 (27/15)	72/51 (22/11)	60/40 (11/4)	46/31 (8/-1)	34/21 (1/-6)
Muskegon	30/17 (-1/-8)	32/18 (0/-8)	42/25 (6/-4)	55/35 (13/2)	67/45 (19/7)	76/54 (24/12)	80/60 (27/16)	78/59 (26/15)	70/51 (21/11)	59/41 (15/5)	46/32 (8/0)	35/23 (2/-5)
Sault Ste. Marie	22/5 (-6/-15)	24/7 (-4/-14)	34/16 (1/-9)	48/29 (9/-2)	63/39 (17/4)	71/46 (22/7)	76/52 (24/11)	74/52 (23/11)	65/45 (18/7)	53/36 (12/2)	39/26 (12/-3)	27/13 (-3/-11)
[4]												

Geology

The geological formation of the state is greatly varied. Primary boulders are found over the entire surface of the Upper Peninsula (being principally of primitive origin), while Secondary deposits cover the entire Lower Peninsula. The Upper Peninsula exhibits Lower Silurian sandstones, limestones, copper and iron bearing rocks, corresponding to the Huronian system of Canada. The central portion of the Lower Peninsula contains coal measures and rocks of the Permo-Carboniferous period. Devonian and sub-Carboniferous deposits are scattered over the entire state.

Demographics

See also: Michigan census statistical areas

Michigan

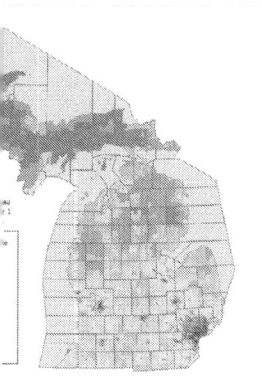

population distribution

Map showing the largest ancestry group in each county

Historical populations		
Census	Pop.	%±
1800	3757	—
1810	4762	26.8%
1820	7452	56.5%
1830	28004	275.8%
1840	212267	658.0%
1850	397654	87.3%
1860	749113	88.4%
1870	1184059	58.1%
1880	1636937	38.2%
1890	2093890	27.9%
1900	2420982	15.6%
1910	2810173	16.1%
1920	3668412	30.5%
1930	4842325	32.0%
1940	5256106	8.5%
1950	6371766	21.2%
1960	7823194	22.8%
1970	8875083	13.4%

1980	9262078	4.4%
1990	9295297	0.4%
2000	9938444	6.9%
Est. 2008	10045697	1.1%

As of July 1, 2008, Michigan had an estimated population of 10,003,422, an increase of 64,930, or 0.7%, since the year 2000. As of 2000, the state had the eighth-largest population in the Union.

The center of population of Michigan is located in Shiawassee County, in the southeastern corner of the civil township of Bennington, which is located directly north of the village of Morrice.

As of 2005-2007 three-year estimate, the state had a foreign-born population of 610,173, or 6% of the total population. In recent years, the foreign-born population in the state has grown. Michigan has the largest Dutch, Finnish, and Macedonian populations in the United States.

As of the 2006-2008 American Community Survey, the racial composition was as follows:

- White: 79.6% (Non-Hispanic Whites: 77.5%)
- Black or African American: 14.0%
- American Indian: 0.5%
- Asian: 2.3%
- Pacific Islander: <0.1%
- Some other race: 1.6%
- Multiracial: 2.0%
- Hispanic or Latino (of any race): 4.0%

Source:

The five largest reported ancestries in Michigan are German (22.4%), African American (14.0%), Irish (12.0%), English (10.6%), and Polish (9.1%).

The large majority of Michigan's population is Caucasian. Americans of European descent live throughout Michigan and most of Metro Detroit. Large European American groups include those of German, Irish, French, and British ancestry. People of Scandinavian descent, especially those of Finnish ancestry, have a notable presence in the Upper Peninsula. Western Michigan is known for the Dutch heritage of many residents (the highest concentration of any state), especially in metropolitan Grand Rapids. Metro Detroit also has residents of Polish and Irish descent.

Dearborn has become the center of a sizeable Arab community, including many Lebanese who immigrated for jobs in the auto industry in the 1920s. About 300,000 people trace their roots to the Middle East which includes. African Americans, who came to Detroit and other northern cities in the Great Migration of the early 20th century, form a majority of the population of the city of Detroit and of other industrial cities, including Flint and Benton Harbor.

An individual from Michigan is called a "Michigander" or "Michiganian". Also at times, but rarely, a "Michiganite". Residents of the Upper Peninsula are sometimes referred to as 'Yoopers" (a phonetic pronunciation of "U.P.ers"), and Upper Peninsula residents sometimes refer to those from the lower as "trolls" (they live below the bridge).

	Demographics of Michigan (csv) [5]				
By race	White	Black	AIAN*	Asian	NHPI*
2000 (total population)	83.05%	14.92%	1.26%	2.10%	0.08%
2000 (Hispanic only)	2.98%	0.22%	0.11%	0.03%	0.01%
2005 (total population)	82.65%	15.05%	1.21%	2.57%	0.08%
2005 (Hispanic only)	3.51%	0.23%	0.11%	0.05%	0.02%
Growth 2000–05 (total population)	1.35%	2.77%	-2.51%	24.24%	12.50%
Growth 2000–05 (non-Hispanic only)	0.66%	2.67%	-2.71%	24.04%	10.70%
Growth 2000–05 (Hispanic only)	19.89%	9.70%	-0.48%	36.87%	20.51%
* AIAN is American Indian or Alaskan Native; NHPI is Native Hawaiian or Pacific Islander					

Religion

The Roman Catholic Church was the only organized religion in Michigan until the 19th century, reflecting the territory's French colonial roots. Detroit's St. Anne's parish, established in 1701, is the second-oldest Catholic parish in the country. French-Canadian Catholics were reduced to a small minority by the influx of Protestants from the United States in the early 19th century. By the mid-19th century, there was a wave of immigration of Catholics from Ireland and, later, from eastern and southern Europe.

Change was rapid in the 19th century. The Lutheran Church was introduced by German and Scandinavian immigrants; Lutheranism is second largest religious denomination in the state. The first Jewish synagogue in the state was Temple Beth El, founded by twelve German Jewish families in Detroit in 1850. Islam was introduced by immigrants from the Near East during the 20th century.

The largest denomination by number of adherents, according to a survey in the year 2000, was the Roman Catholic Church with 2,019,926 parishioners. The largest Protestant denominations were the Lutheran Church–Missouri Synod with 244,231 adherents; followed by the United Methodist Church with 222,269; and the Evangelical Lutheran Church in America with 160,836 adherents. In the same survey, Jewish adherents in the state of Michigan were estimated at 110,000, and Muslims at 80,515.

Economy

See also: List of companies based in Michigan and Economy of metropolitan Detroit

The Bureau of Economic Analysis estimated Michigan's 2004 gross state product at $372 B. Per capita personal income in 2003 was $31,178 and ranked twentieth in the nation. In May 2010, the state's seasonally adjusted unemployment rate was 13.6%, with an actual rate of 12.8% for the month, during a U.S. recession.

Top *Fortune* Companies in Michigan for 2009 (ranked by revenues) with State and U.S. rankings.

State	Corporation	US
1	General Motors	6
2	Ford	7
3	Dow	38
4	Delphi	121
5	Whirlpool	133
6	Ally	147
7	TRW Automotive	169
8	Lear	195
9	Kellogg	210
10	Penske Automotive	225
11	Masco	277
12	Visteon	282
13	DTE Energy	285
14	Arvin Meritor	346
15	CMS Energy	369
16	Stryker	375
17	Autoliv	376
18	Pulte Homes	393
19	Kelly Services	437
20	BorgWarner	453
21	Auto-Owners	476
22	Steelcase	625

23	Borders Group	639
24	Spartan Stores	751
25	Cooper Standard	814
26	Valassis	809
27	Universal Forest	837
28	Affinia Group	853
29	Hayes-Lemmerz	856
30	American Axle	874
31	Herman Miller	897
32	Perrigo	897

Further information:
List of Michigan companies
***Source**: Fortune*

Some of the major industries/products/services include automobiles, cereal products, pizza, information technology, aerospace, military equipment, copper, iron, and furniture. Michigan is the third leading grower of Christmas trees with 60520 acres (245 km^2) of land dedicated to Christmas tree farming. The beverage Vernors was invented in Michigan in 1866, sharing the title of oldest soft drink with Hires Root Beer. Faygo was founded in Detroit on November 4, 1907. Two of the top four pizza chains were founded in Michigan and are headquartered there: Domino's Pizza by Tom Monaghan and Little Caesars Pizza by Mike Ilitch.

Michigan has experienced economic difficulties brought on by volatile stock market disruptions following the September 11, 2001 attacks. This caused a pension and benefit fund crisis for many American companies, including General Motors, Ford, and Chrysler. Since the early 2000s recession and the September 11, 2001 attacks, GM, Ford, and Chrysler have struggled to overcome the benefit funds crisis which followed an ensuing volatile stock market which had caused a severe underfunding condition in the respective U.S. pension and benefit funds (OPEB). Although manufacturing in the state grew 6.6% from 2001 to 2006, the high speculative price of oil became a factor for the U.S. auto industry during the economic crisis of 2008 impacting industry revenues.

During this economic crisis, President George W. Bush extended loans from the Troubled Assets Relief Program (TARP) funds in order to help the GM and Chrysler bridge the recession. In January 2009, President Barack Obama formed an automotive task force in order to help the industry recover and achieve renewed prosperity for the region. With retiree health care costs a significant issue, General Motors, Ford, and Chrysler reached agreements with the United Auto Workers Union to transfer the liabilities for their respective health care and benefit funds to a 501(c)(9) Voluntary Employee Beneficiary Association (VEBA). In spite of these efforts, the severity of the recession required

Detroit's automakers to take additional steps to restructure, including idling many plants. With the U.S. Treasury extending the necessary debtor in possession financing, Chrysler and GM filed separate 'pre-packaged' Chapter 11 restructurings in May and June 2009 respectively.

Michigan ranks fourth nationally in high tech employment with 568,000 high tech workers, which includes 70,000 in the automotive industry. Michigan typically ranks third or fourth in overall Research & development (R&D) expenditures in the United States. Its research and development, which includes automotive, comprises a higher percentage of the state's overall gross domestic product than for any other U.S. state. The state is an important source of engineering job opportunities. The domestic auto industry accounts directly and indirectly for one of every ten jobs in the U.S.

Michigan ranked second nationally in new corporate facilities and expansions in 2004. From 1997 to 2004, Michigan was listed as the only state to top the 10,000 mark for the number of major new developments; however, the effects of the late 2000s recession have slowed the state's economy. In 2008, Michigan ranked third in a survey among the states for luring new business which measured capital investment and new job creation per one million population. In August 2009, Michigan and Detroit's auto industry received $1.36 B in grants from the U.S. Department of Energy for the manufacture of electric vehicle technologies which is expected to generate 6,800 immediate jobs and employ 40,000 in the state by 2020. From 2007 to 2009, Michigan ranked 3rd in the U.S. for new corporate facilities and expansions.

As leading research institutions, the University of Michigan, Michigan State University,and Wayne State University are important partners in the state's economy and the state's University Research Corridor. Michigan's public universities attract more than $1.5 B in research and development grants each year. The National Superconducting Cyclotron Laboratory is located at Michigan State University. Michigan's workforce is well-educated and highly skilled, making it attractive to companies. It has the third highest number of engineering graduates nationally.

Detroit Metropolitan Airport is one of the nation's most recently expanded and modernized airports with six major runways, and large aircraft maintenance facilities capable of servicing and repairing a Boeing 747. Michigan's schools and colleges rank among the nation's best. The state has maintained its early commitment to public education. The state's infrastructure gives it a competitive edge; Michigan has 38 deep water ports. In 2007, Bank of America announced that it would commit $25 billion to community development in Michigan following its acquisition of LaSalle Bank in Troy.

Taxation

Michigan's personal income tax is set to a flat rate of 4.35%. Some cities impose additional income taxes. Michigan's state sales tax is 6%. Property taxes are assessed on the local level, but every property owner's local assessment contributes six mills (six dollars per thousand dollars of property value) to the statutory State Education Tax. In 2007, Michigan repealed its Single Business Tax (SBT) and replaced it with a Michigan Business Tax (MBT) in order to stimulate job growth by reducing taxes for seventy percent of the businesses in the state. According to the Bureau of Economic Analysis, recent growth in Michigan is 0.1%.

Agriculture

A wide variety of commodity crops, fruits, and vegetables are grown in Michigan, making it second only to California among U.S. states in the diversity of its agriculture. The state has 55,000 farms utilizing 10000000 acres (40000 km^2) of land which sold $6.6 billion worth of products in 2008. The most valuable agricultural product is milk. Leading crops include corn, soybeans, flowers, wheat, sugar beets and potatoes. Livestock in the state included 1 million cattle, 1 million hogs, 78,000 sheep and over 3 million chickens. Livestock products accounted for 38% of the value of agricultural products while crops accounted for the majority.

Michigan is the leading U.S. producer of tart cherries, blueberries, pickling cucumbers, red beans and petunias.

Michigan is a leading grower of fruit in the U.S., including blueberries, cherries, apples, grapes, and peaches. These fruits are mainly grown in West Michigan. Michigan produces wines, beers and a multitude of processed food products. Kellogg's cereal is based out of Battle Creek, Michigan and processes many locally grown foods. Thornapple Valley, Ballpark Franks, Koegel's, and Hebrew National sausage companies are all based in Michigan.

Michigan is home to very fertile land in the Flint/Tri-Cities and "Thumb" areas. Products grown there include corn, sugar beets, navy beans, and soy beans. Sugar beet harvesting usually begins the first of October. It takes the sugar factories about five months to process the 3.7 million tons of sugarbeets into 970 million pounds of pure, white sugar. Michigan's largest sugar refiner, Michigan Sugar Company is the largest east of the Mississippi River and the fourth largest in the nation. Michigan Sugar brand names are Pioneer Sugar and the newly incorporated Big Chief Sugar. Potatoes are grown in Northern Michigan, and corn is dominant in Central Michigan. Michigan State University is dedicated to the study of agriculture.

Tourism

See also: List of National Historic Landmarks in Michigan, List of Registered Historic Places in Michigan, and List of museums in Michigan

Michigan has a thriving tourist industry. Visitors spend $17.5 billion per year in the state, supporting 193,000 tourism jobs. Michigan's tourism website ranks among the busiest in the nation. Destinations draw vacationers, hunters, and nature enthusiasts from across the United States and Canada. Michigan is fifty percent forest land, much of it quite remote. The forests, lakes and thousands of miles of beaches are top attractions. Event tourism draws large numbers to occasions like the Tulip Time Festival and the National Cherry Festival.

The Grand Hotel on Mackinac Island is a classic image of Michigan tourism.

In 2006, the Michigan State Board of Education mandated that all public schools in the state hold their first day of school after the Labor Day holiday, in accordance with the new Post Labor Day School law. A survey found that 70% of all tourism business comes directly from Michigan residents, and the Michigan Hotel, Motel, & Resort Association claimed that the shorter summer in between school years cut into the annual tourism season in the state.

Tourism in metropolitan Detroit draws visitors to leading attractions, particularly The Henry Ford, the Detroit Institute of Arts, and the Detroit Zoo, and to sports in Detroit. Other museums include the Detroit Historical Museum, the Charles H. Wright Museum of African American History, museums in the Cranbrook Educational Community, and the Arab American National Museum. The metro area offers four major casinos, MGM Grand Detroit, Greektown, Motor City, and Caesars Windsor in Windsor, Ontario, Canada; moreover, Detroit is the largest American city and metropolitan region to offer casino resorts.

Hunting and fishing are significant industries in the state. Charter boats are based in many Great Lakes cities to fish for salmon, trout, walleye and perch. Michigan ranks first in the nation in licensed hunters (over one million) who contribute $2 billion annually to its economy. Over three-quarters of a million hunters participate in white-tailed deer season alone. Many school districts in rural areas of Michigan cancel school on the opening day of firearm deer season, because of attendance concerns.

Michigan's Department of Natural Resources manages the largest dedicated state forest system in the nation. The forest products industry and recreational users contribute $12 billion and 200,000 associated jobs annually to the state's economy. Public hiking and hunting access has also been secured in extensive commercial forests. The state has highest number of golf courses and registered snowmobiles in the nation.

The state has numerous historical markers, which can themselves become the center of a tour. The Great Lakes Circle Tour is a designated scenic road system connecting all of the Great Lakes and the St. Lawrence River.

With its position in relation to the Great Lakes and the countless ships that have foundered over the many years in which they have been used as a transport route for people and bulk cargo, Michigan is a world-class scuba diving destination. The Michigan Underwater Preserves are 11 underwater areas where wrecks are protected for the benefit of sport divers.

Transportation

Michigan has nine international crossings with Ontario, Canada:

Mackinac Bridge

- Ambassador Bridge, North America's busiest international border crossing the Detroit River
- Blue Water Bridge, a twin-span bridge (Port Huron, Michigan and Point Edward, Ontario, but the larger city of Sarnia, Ontario is usually referred to on the Canadian side.)
- Blue Water Ferry (Marine City, Michigan and Sombra, Ontario)
- Canadian Pacific Railway tunnel.
- Detroit–Windsor Truck Ferry (Detroit, Michigan and Windsor, Ontario)
- Detroit–Windsor Tunnel.
- International Bridge (Sault Ste. Marie, Michigan and Sault Ste. Marie, Ontario)
- St. Clair River Railway Tunnel (Port Huron, Michigan and Sarnia, Ontario)
- Walpole Island Ferry (Algonac, Michigan and Walpole Island First Nation, Ontario

A second international bridge is currently under development between Detroit, Michigan and Windsor, Ontario.

Railroads

See also: List of Michigan railroads and History of railroads in Michigan

Michigan is served by four Class I railroads: the Canadian National Railway, the Canadian Pacific Railway, CSX Transportation, and the Norfolk Southern Railway. These are augmented by several dozen short line railroads. The vast majority of rail service in Michigan is devoted to freight, with Amtrak and various scenic railroads the exceptions.

Main article: Michigan Services

Amtrak passenger rail services the state, connecting many southern and western Michigan cities to Chicago, Illinois. There are plans for commuter rail for Detroit and its suburbs (see SEMCOG Commuter Rail).

Roadways

See also: Michigan Highway System

Interstate 75 is the main thoroughfare between Detroit, Flint, and Saginaw extending north to Sault Sainte Marie and providing access to Sault Sainte Marie, Ontario. The expressway crosses the Mackinac Bridge between the Lower and Upper Peninsulas. Branching highways include I-275 and I-375 in Detroit; I-475 in Flint; and I-675 in Saginaw.

Welcome sign.

Interstate 69 enters the state near the Michigan-Ohio-Indiana border, and it extends to Port Huron and provides access to the Blue Water Bridge crossing into Sarnia, Ontario.

Interstate 94 enters the western end of the state at the Indiana border, and it travels east to Detroit and then northeast to Port Huron and ties in with I-69. I-194 branches off from this freeway in Battle Creek. I-94 is the main artery between Chicago, Illinois and Detroit.

Interstate 96 runs east–west between Detroit and Muskegon. I-496 loops through Lansing. I-196 branches off from this freeway at Grand Rapids and connects to I-94 near Benton Harbor. I-696 branches off from this freeway at Novi and connects to I-94 near St Clair Shores.

U.S. Route 2 enters Michigan at the city of Ironwood and runs east to the town of Crystal Falls, where it turns south and briefly re-enters Wisconsin northwest of Florence. It re-enters Michigan north of Iron Mountain and continues through the Upper Peninsula of Michigan to the cities of Escanaba, Manistique, and St. Ignace. Along the way, it cuts through the Ottawa and Hiawatha National Forests and follows the northern shore of Lake Michigan. Its eastern terminus lies at exit 344 of I-75, just north of the Mackinac Bridge. This is generally regarded as the main route through the Upper Peninsula, although some prefer to travel on M-28 as it tends to save time (U.S. 2 hugs the Lake Michigan shoreline for much of its length.)

Major bridges include the Ambassador Bridge, Blue Water Bridge, Mackinac Bridge, and International Bridge. Michigan also has the Detroit-Windsor Tunnel crossing into Canada.

Airports

See also: List of airports in Michigan

The Detroit Metropolitan Wayne County Airport is Michigan's busiest airport, followed by the Gerald R. Ford International Airport in Grand Rapids.

Important cities and townships

Further information: List of cities, villages, and townships in Michigan

The largest municipalities in Michigan are (according to 2009 census estimates):

The Grand Rapids skyline centered on the Grand River.

A Lansing sunset

Downtown Flint as seen from the Flint River.

The Ann Arbor skyline as seen from Michigan Stadium.

Rank	City	Population
1	Detroit	910,920
2	Grand Rapids	193,710
3	Warren	133,872
4	Sterling Heights	127,176
5	Lansing	113,810
6	Ann Arbor	112,852
7	Flint	111,475
8	Clinton Township	95,990
9	Livonia	89,282
10	Dearborn	84,575

Map showing largest Michigan municipalities.

Other important cities include:

- Battle Creek ("Cereal City U.S.A.", world headquarters of Kellogg Company)
- Benton Harbor / St. Joseph (headquarters of Whirlpool Corporation)
- East Lansing (home of Michigan State University)
- Big Rapids (home of Ferris State University)
- Holland (home of Tulip Time, the largest tulip festival in the U.S.)
- Jackson (headquarters of CMS Energy)
- Kalamazoo (Largest city in southwest Michigan and home to Western Michigan University)
- Manistee (home to the world's largest salt plant, owned by Morton Salt)
- Marquette (largest city in the Upper Peninsula with 19,661 people and home of Northern Michigan University)
- Midland (headquarters of the Dow Chemical Company and the Dow Corning Corporation)
- Mount Pleasant (home of Central Michigan University)
- Muskegon (largest Michigan city on Lake Michigan)
- Pontiac (major automobile manufacturing center, and home of the Pontiac Silverdome)
- Port Huron (major international crossing and home of the Blue Water Bridge)
- Saginaw (the largest of the Tri-Cities, which also consist of Bay City and Midland, and home to Saginaw Valley State University)
- Sault Ste. Marie (home of the Soo Locks and Sault Ste. Marie International Bridge)
- Traverse City ("Cherry Capital of the World", making Michigan the country's largest producer of cherries)
- Ypsilanti (home of Eastern Michigan University)

Half of the wealthiest communities in the state are located in Oakland County, just north of Detroit. Another wealthy community is located just east of the city, in Grosse Pointe. Only three of these cities are located outside of Metro Detroit. The city of Detroit itself, with a per capita income of $14,717, ranks 517th on the list of Michigan locations by per capita income. Benton Harbor is the poorest city in Michigan, with a per capita income of $8,965, while Barton Hills is the richest with a per capita income of $110,683.

Education

See also: List of colleges and universities in Michigan and List of high schools in Michigan

Michigan's education system provides services to 1.6 million K-12 students in public schools. More than 124,000 students attend private schools and an uncounted number are homeschooled under certain legal requirements. The public school system has a $14.5 billion budget in 2008-2009. Michigan has a number of public universities spread throughout the state and a numerous private colleges as well. Michigan State University has one of the largest enrollments of any U.S. school. Michigan State and University of Michigan are leading research institutions.

Professional sports

Main article: List of Michigan professional sports teams

Michigan's major-league sports teams include: Detroit Tigers baseball team, Detroit Lions football team, Detroit Red Wings ice hockey team, and the Detroit Pistons men's basketball team.

The Pistons played at Detroit's Cobo Arena until 1978 and at the Pontiac Silverdome until 1988 when they moved into the Palace of Auburn Hills. The Detroit Lions played at Tiger Stadium in Detroit until 1974, then moved to the Pontiac Silverdome where they played for 27 years between 1975-2002 before moving to Ford Field in Detroit in 2002. The Detroit Tigers played at Tiger Stadium (Detroit) (formerly known as Navin Field and Briggs Stadium) from 1912 to 1999. In 2000 they moved to Comerica Park. The Red Wings played at Olympia Stadium before moving to Joe Louis Arena in 1979.

Thirteen-time Grand Slam champion Serena Williams was born in Saginaw. The Michigan International Speedway is the site of NASCAR races and Detroit was formerly the site of a Grand Prix race. Michigan is home to one of the major canoeing marathons: the 120-mile (190 km) Au Sable River Canoe Marathon. Professional hockey got its start in Houghton, when the Portage Lakers were formed.

State symbols and nicknames

Michigan is, by tradition, known as "The Wolverine State," and the University of Michigan takes the wolverine as its mascot. The association is well and long established: for example, many Detroiters volunteered to fight during the American Civil War and George Armstrong Custer, who led the Michigan Brigade, called them the "Wolverines". The origins of this association are obscure; it may derive from a busy trade in wolverine furs in Sault Ste. Marie in the 18th century or may recall a disparagement intended to compare early settlers in Michigan with the vicious mammal. Wolverines are, however, extremely rare in Michigan. A sighting in February 2004 near Ubly was the first confirmed sighting in Michigan in 200 years. The animal was found dead in 2010.

- State nicknames: *Wolverine State, Great Lakes State, Mitten State, Water-Winter Wonderland*
- State motto: *Si quaeris peninsulam amoenam circumspice* (Latin: If you seek a pleasant peninsula, look about you) adopted in 1835 on the coat-of-arms, but never as an official 'motto'. This is a paraphrase of the epitaph of British architect Sir Christopher Wren about his masterpiece, St. Paul's Cathedral.
- State song: *My Michigan* (official since 1937, but disputed amongst residents), *Michigan, My Michigan* (Unofficial State Song, since the civil war)
- State bird: American Robin (since 1931)
- State animal: Wolverine (traditional)
- State game animal: White-tailed deer (since 1997)
- State fish: Brook trout (since 1965)
- State reptile: Painted Turtle (since 1995)
- State fossil: Mastodon (since 2000)
- State flower: Apple blossom (adopted in 1897, official in 1997)
- State wildflower: Dwarf Lake Iris (since 1998). Known as *Iris lacustris*, it is a federally listed threatened species.
- State tree: White pine (since 1955)
- State stone: Petoskey stone (since 1965). It is composed of fossilized coral (*Hexagonaria pericarnata*) from long ago when the middle of the continent was covered with a shallow sea.
- State gem: Isle Royale greenstone (since 1973). Also called *chlorastrolite* (literally "green star stone"), the mineral is found on Isle Royale and the Keweenaw peninsula.
- State Quarter: U.S. coin issued in 2004 with the Michigan motto "Great Lake State."
- State soil: Kalkaska Sand (since 1990), ranges in color from black to yellowish brown, covers nearly 1000000-acre (4000 km^2) in 29 counties.

Sister states

- Shiga Prefecture, Japan
- Sichuan Province, Peoples Republic of China

See also

- Outline of Michigan
- Index of Michigan-related articles
- USS Michigan

Further reading

- Bald, F. Clever, *Michigan in Four Centuries* (1961)[i]
- Browne, William P. and - Kenneth VerBurg. *Michigan Politics & Government: Facing Change in a Complex State* University of Nebraska Press. 1995.
- Bureau of Business Research, Wayne State U. *Michigan Statistical Abstract* (1987).
- Clarke Historical Library, Central Michigan University, Bibliographies for Michigan by region, counties, etc. [6].
- Dunbar, Willis F. and George S. May. *Michigan: A History of the Wolverine State* (1995) excerpt and text search [7]
- Michigan, State of. *Michigan Manual* (annual), elaborate detail on state government.
- Press, Charles et al., *Michigan Political Atlas* (1984).
- Public Sector Consultants. *Michigan in Brief: An Issues Handbook* (annual)
- Rich, Wilbur. *Coleman Young and Detroit Politics: From Social Activist to Power Broker* (Wayne State University Press, 1988).
- Rubenstein, Bruce A. and Lawrence E. Ziewacz. *Michigan: A History of the Great Lakes State.* (2nd ed. 2008)
- Sisson, Richard, Ed. *The American Midwest: An Interpretive Encyclopedia* (2006)
- Weeks, George, *Stewards of the State: The Governors of Michigan* (Historical Society of Michigan, 1987).

External links

- State of Michigan government website [8]
- Energy Data & Statistics for Michigan [9]
- Info Michigan, detailed information on 630 cities [10]
- Michigan Historic Markers [11]
- Michigan History Magazine [12]
- Michigan Lighthouse Chronology - Clark Historical Library [13]
- Michigan State Guide from the Library of Congress [14]
- Michigan Official Travel Site [15]
- Michigan travel guide from Wikitravel
- Michigan [16] at the Open Directory Project
- Michigan State Fact Sheet [17] from the U.S. Department of Agriculture
- Michigan Underwater Preserves Council [18]
- The Michigan Municipal League [19]
- USGS real-time, geographic, and other scientific resources of Michigan [20]

> **Bold Faced** States/Provinces bound Michigan completely over water.
>
> ***Bold Italicized*** States bound Michigan partially over water.
>
> None of Michigan's neighbors border them completely over land. Even Indiana and Ohio have small portions of border that is over one of the Great Lakes, Lake Michigan (Indiana) and Lake Erie (Ohio).
>
> Wisconsin's border with Michigan is mainly over water except for most of their border with the Upper Peninsula, which is over land and to the southwest.

1. REDIRECT Template:Navboxes

Geographical coordinates: 44°20′N 85°35′W

frr:Michigan pnb:مشیگن

History of Michigan

The **History of Michigan** is divided into the following articles.

See also Timeline of Michigan history.

Main article: Michigan

Aerial photo of Soo Locks and International Bridge displaying the historic relationships Michigan has with the Great Lakes and Canada.

Before 1776

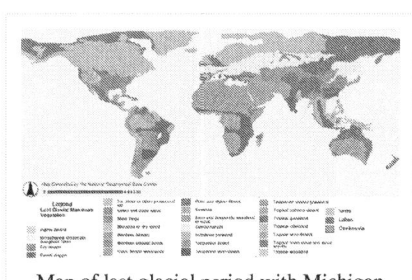

Map of last glacial period with Michigan and Great Lakes Basin entirely covered by an ice sheet.

Thousands of years before the arrival of the first Europeans, several indigenous tribes lived in what is today the state of Michigan. They included the Ojibwa, Menominee, Miami, Ottawa, and Potawatomi, who were part of the Algonquian family of Amerindians, as well as the Wyandot, who were from the Iroquoian family and lived in the area of present-day Detroit. It is estimated that the native population at the time the first European arrived was 15,000.

The first white explorer to visit Michigan was the Frenchman Étienne Brûlé in 1620, who began his expedition from Quebec City on the orders of Samuel de Champlain and traveled as far as the Upper Peninsula. Afterward, the area became part of Louisiana, one of the large colonial provinces of New France. The first permanent European settlement in Michigan was founded in 1668 at Sault Ste. Marie by Jacques Marquette, a French missionary.

The French built several trading posts, forts, and villages in Michigan during the late 17th century. Among them, the most important was Fort Pontchartrain du Détroit, established by Antoine de Lamothe Cadillac. This grew to become Detroit. Up until this time, French activities in the region were limited to hunting, trapping, trading with and the conversion of local Indians, and some limited subsistence agriculture. By 1760, the Michigan countryside had only a few hundred white inhabitants.

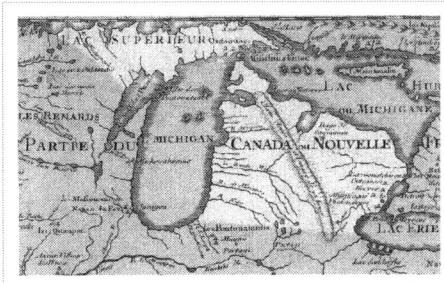

Michigan in 1718, Guillaume de L'Isle map, approximate state area highlighted.

Territorial disputes between French and British colonists helped start the French and Indian War as part of the larger Seven Years' War, which took place from 1754 to 1763 and resulted in the defeat of France. As part of the Treaty of Paris, the French ceded all of their North American colonies east of the Mississippi River to Britain. Thus the future Michigan was handed over to the British. In 1774, the area was made part of Quebec. It continued to be sparsely populated. Regional growth proceeded slowly because the British were more interested in the fur trade and peace with the natives than in settlement of the area.

From 1776 to 1837

During the American Revolutionary War, the local European population, who were primarily American colonists that supported independence, rebelled against Britain. The British, with the help of local tribes, continually attacked American settlements in the region starting in 1776 and conquered Detroit. In 1781, Spanish raiders led by a French Captain Eugene Poure travelled by river and overland from St Louis, liberated British-held Fort St Joseph, and handed authority over the settlement to the Americans the following day. The war ended with the signing of the Treaty of Paris in 1783, and Michigan passed into the control of the newly formed United States of America. In 1787, the region became part of the Northwest Territory. The British, however, continued to occupy Detroit and other fortifications and did not definitively leave the area until after the implementation of the Jay Treaty in 1796.

Unfinished contemporaneous painting of the American diplomatic negotiators of the Treaty of Paris which brought official conclusion to the Revolutionary War and gave possession of Michigan and other territory to the new United States.

The land which is now Michigan was made part of Indiana Territory in 1800. Most was declared as Michigan Territory in 1805, including all of the Lower Peninsula. During the War of 1812, British forces from Canada captured Detroit and Fort Mackinac early on, giving them a strategic advantage and encouraging native revolt against the United States. American troops retook Detroit in 1813 and Fort Mackinac was returned to the Americans at the end of the war in 1815.

Over the 1810s, the indigenous Ojibwa, Ottawa, and Potawatomi tribes increasingly decided to oppose white settlement and sided with the British against the U.S. government.

After their defeat in the War of 1812, the tribes were forced to sell all of their land claims to the US federal government by the Treaty of Saginaw and the Treaty of Chicago. After the war, the government built forts in some of the northwest territory, such as at Sault Ste. Marie. In the 1820s the US government assigned Indian agents to work with the tribes, including arranging land cessions and relocation. They forced most of the Native Americans to relocate from Michigan to Indian reservations further west.

During the 1820s, the population of Michigan Territory grew rapidly, largely because of the opening of the Erie Canal in 1825. Its connection of the navigable waters of the middle Great Lakes to those of the Atlantic Ocean dramatically sped up transportation between the eastern states and the less-inhabited western territories. The canal created new possibilities for transport of produce and goods to market, as well as easing passage of migrants to the west.

Michigan's oldest university, the University of Michigan was founded in Detroit in 1817 and was later moved to its present location in Ann Arbor. The state's oldest cultural instititon, the Historical Society of Michigan, was established by territorial governor Lewis Cass and explorer Henry Schoolcraft in 1828.

Rising settlement prompted the elevation of Michigan Territory to that of the present-day state. In 1835, the federal government enacted a law that would have created a State of Michigan. A territorial dispute with Ohio over the Toledo Strip, a stretch of land including the city of Toledo, delayed the final accession of statehood. The disputed zone became part of Ohio by the order of a revised bill passed by the U.S. Congress and signed into law by President Andrew Jackson which also gave compensation to Michigan in the form of control of the Upper Peninsula. On January 26, 1837, Michigan became the 26th state of the Union.

From 1837 to 1900

During the early 1840s, large deposits of copper and iron ores were discovered on the Upper Peninsula.

Michigan actively participated in the American Civil War sending thousands of volunteers. After the war, the local economy became more varied and began to prosper economically. During the 1870s, the lumber industry, dairy farming and diversified industry grew rapidly in the state. The population doubled between 1870 and 1890.

Toward the end of the century, the state government established a state school system on the German model, with public schools, high schools, normal schools or colleges for training teachers of lower grades, and colleges for classical academic studies and professors. It dedicated more funds to public education than did any other state in the nation. Within a few years, it established four-year curriculums at its normal colleges, and was the first state to establish a full college program for them.

Railroads have been vital in the history of the population and trade of rough and finished goods in the state of Michigan. While some coastal settlements had previously existed, the population, commercial, and industrial growth of the state further bloomed with the establishment of the railroad.

1900 to 1941

During the early 20th century, manufacturing industries became the main source of revenue for Michigan – in large part, because of the automobile. In 1899, the Olds Motor Vehicle Company opened a factory in Detroit. In 1903, Ford Motor Company was also founded there. With the mass production of the Ford Model T, Detroit became the world capital of the auto industry. General Motors is based in Detroit, Chrysler is located in Rochester Hills, and Ford is headquartered in nearby Dearborn. Both corporations constructed large industrial complexes in the Detroit metropolitan area, exemplified by the River Rouge Plant, which have made Michigan a national leader in manufacturing since the 1910s. This industrial base produced greatly during World War I, filling a huge demand for military vehicles.

Photo of workers occupying a General Motors car body factory during the Flint Sit-Down Strike which spurred the organization of unions in the U.S. auto industry.

Jackson was home to one of the first car industry developments. Even before Detroit began building cars on assembly lines, Jackson was busy making parts for cars and putting them together in 1901. By 1910, the auto industry became Jackson's main industry. Over twenty different cars were once made in Jackson. Including: Reeves, Jaxon, Jackson, CarterCar, Orlo, Whiting, Butcher and Gage, Buick, Janney, Globe, Steel Swallow, C.V.I., Imperial, Ames-Dean, Cutting, Standard Electric, Duck, Briscoe, Argo, Hollier, Hackett, Marion-Handly, Gem, Earl, Wolverine, and Kaiser-Darrin. Today the auto industry remains one of the largest employers of skilled machine operators in Jackson County.

With the expansion of industry, hundreds of thousands of migrants from the South and immigrants from eastern and southern Europe were attracted to Detroit. In a short time, it became the fourth largest city in the country - housing shortages persisted for years even as new housing was developed throughout the city. Ethnic immigrant enclaves rapidly developed where churches, bakeries and businesses supported unique communities. A guide to the city written in the 1930s noted that there were students speaking more than 35 languages in the public schools. Ethnic festivals were a regular part of the city's culture. At the same time, such rapid social change created an environment in which the second Ku Klux Klan recruited members in the city. Their influence was at a peak in 1925, but membership fell quickly after that.

The Great Depression caused severe economic hardship in Michigan. Thousands of auto industry workers were dismissed along with other workers from several sectors of the state economy. The financial suffering was aggravated by the fact that remaining copper reserves in the state lay deep underground. With the discovery of copper finds in other states located in less deep rock layers, local mining fell sharply and resulted in unemployment for thousands of miners. The federal government took several measures to try to diminish the negative effects. It created the Civilian Conservation Corps, a work relief program that started hiring thousands of unemployed young men for jobs like maintenance and cleaning. The Works Progress Administration was another federal agency which hired more than 500,000 unemployed people in Michigan alone to construct major public works such as roads, buildings, and dams.

During this time, United Auto Workers was founded to represent automotive industry employees. This labor union pressured Michigan auto companies to hire for contract only workers who were union members and wanted to handle negotiations between managers and workers. Ford and General Motors became the main targets of the UAW, and continuous strikes, the most important of which was the Flint Sit-Down Strike, forced both companies to recognize the existence of the union. Today, the UAW is one of the largest unions in the United States and has represented all of the employed workers of domestic automobile companies since 1941.

After 1941

The entry of the United States into World War II the same year ended the economic contraction in Michigan. Wartime required the large-scale production of weapons and military vehicles, leading to a massive number of new jobs being filled. After the end of the war, both the automotive and copper mining industries recovered.

Starting during WWI, the Great Migration fueled the movement of thousands of African-Americans from the South to industrial jobs in Michigan and, especially, Detroit. Migration of white southerners to the city increased the volatility of change. Population increases continued with industrial expansion during WWII and afterward. African Americans contributed to a new vibrant urban culture, with expansion of new music, food and culture.

The postwar years were initially a prosperous time for industrial workers, who achieved middle-class livelihoods. These were the years of the creation and popularity of Motown Records. By late mid-century, however, deindustrialization and restructuring cost many jobs. The economy suffered and the city postponed needed changes. Neglect of social problems and urban decline fed racial conflicts. In 1967 the 12th St. Riot erupted, lasting eight days, causing 25 million dollars in damages, and resulting in 43 deaths. The violence caused many people to leave the city who could, to avoid future problems.

Gerald Ford, a politician from Grand Rapids who was elected to the House of Representatives thirteen times and also served as House Minority Leader and then Vice President, became the 38th President of the United States after the resignation of Richard Nixon.

The 1973 Oil Crisis caused economic recession in the United States and greatly affected the Michigan economy. Afterward, automobile companies in the United States faced greater multinational competition, especially from Japan. As a consequence, domestic auto makers enacted cost-cutting measures to remain competitive at home and abroad. Unemployment rates rose dramatically in the state.

Throughout the 1970s, Michigan possessed the highest unemployment rate of any U.S. state. Large spending cuts to education and public health were repeatedly made in an attempt to reduce growing state budget deficits. A strengthening of the auto industry and an increase in tax revenue stabilized government and household finances in the 1980s. Increasing competition by Japanese and South Korean auto companies continues to challenge the state economy, which depends heavily on the automobile industry. Since the late 1980s, the government of Michigan has actively sought to attract new industries, thus reducing economic reliance on a single sector.

Further reading

- Bald, F. Clever, *Michigan in Four Centuries* (1961)/
- Browne, William P. and - Kenneth VerBurg. *Michigan Politics & Government: Facing Change in a Complex State* University of Nebraska Press. 1995.
- Bureau of Business Research, Wayne State U. *Michigan Statistical Abstract* (1987).
- Clarke Historical Library, Central Michigan University, Bibliographies for Michigan by region, counties, etc. [6].
- Dunbar, Willis F. and George S. May. *Michigan: A History of the Wolverine State* (1995) excerpt and text search [7]
- Michigan, State of. *Michigan Manual* (annual), elaborate detail on state government.
- *Michigan Historical Review* Central Michigan University (quarterly).
- Nolan, Alan T. *The Iron Brigade: A Military History* (1994), famous Civil War combat unit
- Press, Charles et al., *Michigan Political Atlas* (1984).
- Public Sector Consultants. *Michigan in Brief. An Issues Handbook* (annual)
- Rich, Wilbur. *Coleman Young and Detroit Politics: From Social Activist to Power Broker* (Wayne State University Press, 1988).
- Rubenstein, Bruce A. and Lawrence E. Ziewacz. *Michigan: A History of the Great Lakes State.* (2002)
- Sisson, Richard, Ed. *The American Midwest: An Interpretive Encyclopedia* (2006)
- Trap. Paul, and Larry Wagenaar. *Michigan History Directory of Historical Societies, Museums, Archives, Historic Sites, Agencies and Commissions* (12th Ed. 2008)
- Weeks, George, *Stewards of the State: The Governors of Michigan* (Historical Society of Michigan, 1987).

See also

Main article: Historical outline of Michigan

- Algonquian peoples
- European colonization of the Americas
- History of Detroit
- History of Ford Motor Company
- History of General Motors
- History of railroads in Michigan
- History of the Midwestern United States
- International Boundary Waters Treaty
- Inland Northern American English

- Northwest Ordinance
- List of Michigan county name etymologies
- List of museums in Michigan
- Sixty Years' War
- Timeline of Michigan history
- Timeline of the Toledo Strip/War
- War of 1812

External links

- Historical Society of Michigan [1]
- Official State of Michigan History, Arts & Libraries homepage (MHAL) [2]

Geography of Michigan

Michigan consists of two peninsulas that lie between 82°30' to about 90°30' west longitude, and are separated by the Straits of Mackinac, and some nearby islands. With the exception of two small areas that are drained by the Mississippi River by way of the Wisconsin River in the Upper Peninsula and by way of the Kankakee-Illinois River in the Lower Peninsula, Michigan is drained by the Great Lakes-St. Lawrence watershed and is the only state with the majority of its land thus drained.

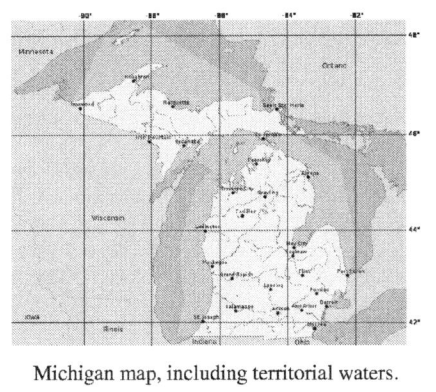

Michigan map, including territorial waters.

Great Lakes

The Great Lakes that border Michigan from east to west are Lake Erie, Lake Huron, Lake Michigan and Lake Superior. Because of the lakes, Michigan has more lighthouses than any other state.[citation needed] The state is bounded on the south by the states of Ohio and Indiana, sharing land and water boundaries with both. Michigan's western boundaries are almost entirely water boundaries, from south to north, with Illinois and Wisconsin in Lake

Michigan; then a land boundary with Wisconsin and the Upper Peninsula, that is principally demarcated by the Menominee and Montreal Rivers; then water boundaries again, in Lake Superior, with Wisconsin and Minnesota to the west, capped around by the Canadian province of Ontario to the north and east.

The northern boundary then runs completely through Lake Superior, from the western boundary with Minnesota to a point north of and around Isle Royale, thence traveling southeastward through the lake in a reasonably straight line to the Sault Ste. Marie area. In Southeastern Michigan there is a water boundary with Canada along the entire lengths of the St Clair River, Lake St. Clair (including the First Nation reserve of Walpole Island) and the Detroit River). The southeastern boundary ends in the western end of Lake Erie with a three-way convergence of Michigan, Ohio and Ontario.

Aerial View of Sleeping Bear Dunes

The Pointe Mouillee State Game Area

Tahquamenon Falls in the Upper Peninsula of Michigan.

Michigan encompasses 58,110 square miles (150,504 km²) of land, 38,575 square miles (99,909 km²) of Great Lakes waters and 1,305 square miles (3,380 km²) of inland waters. Only Alaska has more territorial water. At a total of 97,990 square miles (253,793 km²), Michigan is the largest state east of the Mississippi River (inclusive of its territorial waters). Michigan claims a land area of 58110 square miles (150500 km^2) of land and 97990 sq mi (253790 km^2) total, making it the tenth largest state, but the U.S. Census Bureau claims only 56803.82 sq mi (147121.22 km^2) of land and 96716.11 sq mi (250493.57 km^2) total, making it the eleventh largest. Michigan forestland covers nearly 52% of the state at 19300000 acres (78000 km^2).

Upper Peninsula

The heavily forested Upper Peninsula is relatively mountainous in the west. The Porcupine Mountains, which are part of one of the oldest mountain chains in the world, rise to an altitude of almost 2,000 feet (610 m) above sea level and form the watershed between the streams flowing into Lake Superior and Lake Michigan. The surface on either side of this range is rugged. The state's highest point, in the Huron Mountains northwest of Marquette, is Mount Arvon at 1,979 feet (603 m). The peninsula is as large as Connecticut, Delaware, Massachusetts, and Rhode Island combined but has fewer than 330,000 inhabitants. They are sometimes called "Yoopers" (from "U.P.'ers"), and their speech (the "Yooper dialect") has been heavily influenced by the numerous Scandinavian and Canadian immigrants who settled the area during the lumbering and mining boom of the late nineteenth century.

The geographic orientation of Michigan's peninsulas makes for a long distance between the ends of the state. Ironwood, in the far western Upper Peninsula, lies 630 highway miles (1,015 km) from Lambertville in the Lower Peninsula's southeastern corner. The geographic isolation of the Upper Peninsula from Michigan's political and population centers makes the U.P. culturally and economically distinct. Occasionally U.P. residents have called for secession from Michigan and establishment as a new state to be called "Superior."

Lower Peninsula

Little Traverse Bay at sunset, viewed from Petoskey

The Lower Peninsula, shaped like a mitten, is 277 miles (446 km) long from north to south and 195 miles (314 km) from east to west and occupies nearly two-thirds of the state's land area. The surface of the peninsula is generally level, broken by conical hills and glacial moraines usually not more than a few hundred feet tall. It is divided by a low water divide running north and south. The larger portion of the state is on the west of this and gradually slopes toward Lake Michigan. The highest point in the Lower Peninsula is either Briar Hill at 1,705 feet (520 m), or one of several points nearby in the vicinity of Cadillac. The lowest point is the surface of Lake Erie at 571 feet (174 m).

A feature of Michigan that gives it the distinct shape of a mitten is the Thumb. This peninsula projects out into Lake Huron and the Saginaw Bay. The geography of the Thumb is mainly flat with a few rolling hills. Other peninsulas of Michigan include the Keweenaw Peninsula, making up the Copper Country region of the state. The Leelanau Peninsula lies in the Northern Lower Michigan region. *See Also Michigan Regions*

Lakes

Little Sable Point Light south of Pentwater, Michigan.

Numerous lakes and marshes mark both peninsulas, and the coast is much indented. Keweenaw Bay, Whitefish Bay, and the Big and Little Bays De Noc are the principal indentations on the Upper Peninsula. The Grand and Little Traverse, Thunder, and Saginaw bays indent the Lower Peninsula After Alaska, Michigan has the longest shoreline of any state—3,288 miles (5,326 km). An additional 1,056 miles (1,699 km) can be added if islands are included. This roughly equals the length of the Atlantic Coast from Maine to Florida.

The state has numerous large islands, the principal ones being the Manitou, Beaver, and Fox groups in Lake Michigan; Isle Royale and Grande Isle in Lake Superior; Drummond, Marquette, Bois Blanc, and Mackinac islands in Lake Huron; and Neebish and Sugar islands in St. Mary's River. Michigan has about 150 lighthouses, the most of any U.S. state. The first lighthouses in Michigan were built between 1818 and 1822. They were built to project light at night and to serve as a landmark during the day to safely guide the passenger ships and freighters traveling the Great Lakes. See Lighthouses in the United States.

The state's rivers are small, short and shallow, and few are navigable. The principal ones include the Au Sable, Thunder Bay, Cheboygan, and Saginaw, all of which flow into Lake Huron; the Ontonagon, and Tahquamenon, which flow into Lake Superior; and the St. Joseph, Kalamazoo, Grand, Muskegon, Manistee, and Escanaba, which flow into Lake Michigan. The state has 11,037 inland lakes and 38,575 square miles (62,067 km²) of Great Lakes waters and rivers in addition to 1305 square miles (3380 km^2) of inland water. No point in Michigan is more than six miles (10 km) from an inland lake or more than 85 miles (137 km) from one of the Great Lakes.

Protected lands

See also: List of Michigan state parks

The state is home to one national park: Isle Royale National Park, located in Lake Superior, about 30 miles (48 km) southeast of Thunder Bay, Ontario. Other national protected areas in the state include: Keweenaw National Historical Park, Pictured Rocks National Lakeshore, Sleeping Bear Dunes National Lakeshore, Huron National Forest, Manistee National Forest, Hiawatha National Forest, Ottawa National Forest, Fumee Lake Natural Area and Father Marquette National Memorial. The largest section of the North Country National Scenic Trail also passes through Michigan.

With 78 state parks, 19 state recreation areas, and 6 state forests, Michigan has the largest state park and state forest system of any state. These parks and forests include Holland State Park, Mackinac Island State Park, Au Sable State Forest, and Mackinaw State Forest.

Climate

Michigan has a humid continental climate, although there are two distinct regions. The southern and central parts of the Lower Peninsula (south of Saginaw Bay and from the Grand Rapids area southward) have a warmer climate (Koppen climate classification *Dfa*) with hot summers and cold winters. The northern part of Lower Peninsula and the entire Upper Peninsula has a more severe climate (Koppen *Dfb*), with warm, but shorter summers and longer, cold to very cold winters. Some parts of the state average high temperatures below freezing from December through February, and into early March in the far northern parts. During the winter through the middle of February the state is frequently subjected to heavy lake-effect snow. The state averages from 30-40 inches (75–100 cm) of precipitation annually.

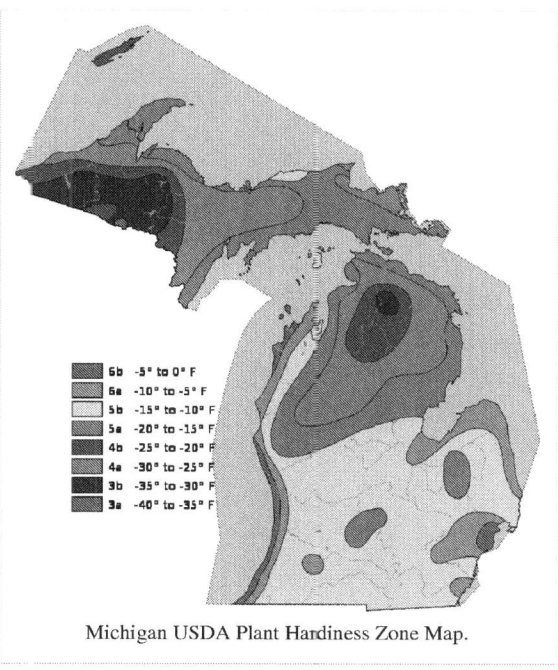

Michigan USDA Plant Hardiness Zone Map.

The entire state averages 30 days of thunderstorm activity per year. These can be severe, especially in the southern part of the state. The state averages 17 tornadoes per year, which are more common in the extreme southern portion of the state. Portions of the southern border have been nearly as vulnerable historically as parts of Tornado Alley. Farther north, in the Upper Peninsula, tornadoes are rare.

Monthly Normal High and Low Temperatures For Various Michigan Cities in °F(°C)												
City	**Jan**	**Feb**	**Mar**	**Apr**	**May**	**Jun**	**Jul**	**Aug**	**Sep**	**Oct**	**Nov**	**Dec**
Detroit	31/18 (-1/-8)	34/20 (1/-7)	45/28 (7/-2)	58/38 (14/3)	70/49 (21/9)	79/59 (26/15)	83/64 (28/18)	81/62 (27/17)	74/54 (23/12)	61/42 (16/6)	48/34 (9/1)	36/23 (2/-5)
Flint	29/13 (-2/-11)	32/15 (0/-9)	43/24 (6/-4)	56/35 (13/2)	69/45 (21/7)	78/55 (26/13)	82/59 (28/15)	80/57 (27/14)	72/49 (22/9)	60/39 (16/4)	46/30 (8/-1)	34/19 (1/-7)
Grand Rapids	29/16 (-2/-9)	33/17 (1/-8)	43/26 (6/-3)	57/36 (14/2)	70/47 (21/8)	78/55 (26/13)	82/60 (28/16)	80/59 (27/15)	72/51 (22/11)	60/40 (11/4)	46/31 (8/-1)	34/21 (1/-6)
Lansing	29/14 (-2/-10)	33/15 (1/-9)	44/24 (7/-4)	57/34 (14/1)	69/45 (21/7)	78/54 (26/12)	82/58 (28/14)	80/57 (27/14)	72/49 (22/9)	60/39 (16/4)	46/30 (8/-1)	34/20 (1/-7)
Marquette	20/3 (-7/-16)	24/5 (-4/-15)	33/14 (1/-10)	46/27 (8/-3)	62/39 (17/4)	70/43 (21/9)	75/54 (24/12)	73/52 (23/11)	63/44 (17/7)	51/34 (11/1)	35/22 (2/-6)	24/10 (-4/-12)

Muskegon	30/17 (-1/-8)	32/18 (0/-8)	42/25 (6/-4)	55/35 (13/2)	67/45 (19/7)	76/54 (24/12)	80/60 (27/16)	78/59 (26/15)	70/51 (21/11)	59/41 (15/5)	46/32 (8/0)	35/23 (2/-5)
Sault Ste Marie	22/5 (-6/-15)	24/7 (-4/-14)	34/16 (1/-9)	48/29 (9/-2)	63/39 (17/4)	71/46 (22/7)	76/52 (24/11)	74/52 (23/11)	65/45 (18/7)	53/36 (12/2)	39/26 (12/-3)	27/13 (-3/-11)
[4]												

Geology

The geological formation of the state is greatly varied. Primary boulders are found over the entire surface of the Upper Peninsula (being principally of primitive origin), while Secondary deposits cover the entire Lower Peninsula. The Upper Peninsula exhibits Lower Silurian sandstones, limestones, copper and iron bearing rocks, corresponding to the Huronian system of Canada. The central portion of the Lower Peninsula contains coal measures and rocks of the Permo-Carboniferous period. Devonian and sub-Carboniferous deposits are scattered over the entire state.

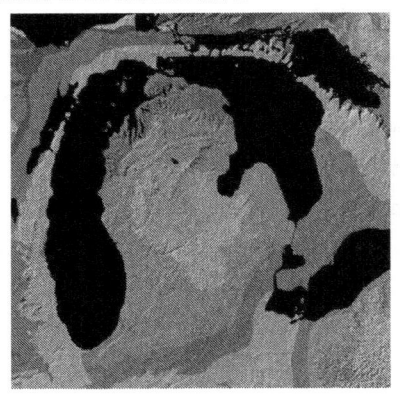

Geologic map of the Michigan Basin.

The soil is of a varied composition and in large areas is very fertile, especially in the south. However, the Upper Peninsula for the most part is rocky and mountainous, and the soil is unsuitable for agriculture. The climate is tempered by the proximity of the lakes and is much milder than in other locales with the same latitude. The principal forest trees include basswood, maple, elm, sassafras, butternut, walnut, poplar, hickory, oak, willow, pine, birch, beech, hemlock, witchhazel, tamarack, cedar, locust, dogwood, and ash.

List of Michigan state parks

This is a list of **Michigan state parks and related protected areas** under Michigan Department of Natural Resources and Environment (DNRE) jurisdiction. DNRE also operates 16 state harbors on the Great Lakes. Michigan's state parks system was started in 1919 and now contains 98 parks and recreation areas covering 285,000 acres (1,150 km²). There are 13,500 campsites in 142 campgrounds and 879 miles (1400 km) of trails. The parks received 21.2 million visitors in 2008.

Lake of the Clouds in Porcupine Mountains Wilderness State Park

Two Michigan state parks pre-date the creation of the park system in 1919. Michigan's first state park, Mackinac Island State Park, was created in 1895. It had served as the nation's second national park from 1875. In 1909 Michilimackinac State Park was created in nearby Mackinaw City. Both these parks, along with Historic Mill Creek State Park are under the jurisdiction of the Mackinac Island State Park Commission.

DNRE operates 746 boat launches on 57000 acres (230 km^2) of designated public water access sites. It also operates 16 "harbors of refuge" as well as providing support for the other 61 harbors in the system. The harbors of refuge are approximately 30 miles (50 km) apart along the Great Lakes shoreline to provide shelter from storms and often provide boat launches and supplies. There are 11 state underwater preserves covering 2450 square miles (6300 km^2) of Great Lakes bottomland and ten of them have a maritime museum or interpretive center in a nearby coastal community.

The state forest system consists of 4000000 acres (20000 km^2) of primarily working forest but also includes 138 campgrounds (including a dozen equestrian campgrounds). The Michigan state game and wildlife areas encompass more than 340000 acres (1400 km^2). DNRE also oversee the trail systems in the state. This includes 880 miles (1400 km) of non-motorized trails, 1145 miles (1800 km) of rail-trails, 3193 miles (5100 km) of off-road vehicle (ORV) routes and 6216 miles (10000 km) of snowmobile trails.

For a discussion of all protected areas in Michigan under all jurisdictions, see Protected areas of Michigan.

State parks

- Algonac State Park
- Aloha State Park
- Baraga State Park
- Bewabic State Park
- Brimley State Park
- Burt Lake State Park
- Cambridge Junction Historic State Park
- Cheboygan State Park
- Clear Lake State Park
- Coldwater Lake State Park
- Craig Lake State Park
- Dodge #4 State Park
- Duck Lake State Park
- Fayette Historic State Park
- Fisherman's Island State Park
- Fort Wilkins Historic State Park

Grand Mere State Park

- Grand Haven State Park
- Grand Mere State Park
- Harrisville State Park
- Hart-Montague Trail State Park
- Hartwick Pines State Park
- Hayes State Park
- Historic Mill Creek State Park
- Hoeft State Park (P.H. Hoeft)
- Hoffmaster State Park (P.J. Hoffmaster)
- Holland State Park
- Indian Lake State Park
- Interlochen State Park
- Kal-Haven Trail State Park
- Lake Gogebic State Park
- Lakelands Trail State Park
- Lakeport State Park
- Leelanau State Park

Holland State Park

- Ludington State Park
- Mackinac Island State Park and Fort Mackinac
- Maybury State Park
- McLain State Park (F.J. McLain)
- Mears State Park
- Meridian-Baseline State Park
- Colonial Michilimackinac and Old Mackinac Point Lighthouse
- Mitchell State Park
- Muskallonge Lake State Park
- Muskegon State Park
- Negwegon State Park
- Newaygo State Park
- North Higgins Lake State Park
- Onaway State Park
- Orchard Beach State Park
- Otsego Lake State Park
- Palms Book State Park
- Petoskey State Park
- Porcupine Mountains State Park
- Port Crescent State Park
- Sanilac Petroglyphs Historic State Park
- Saugatuck Dunes State Park
- Seven Lakes State Park
- Silver Lake State Park
- Sleeper State Park
- Sleepy Hollow State Park
- South Higgins Lake State Park
- Sterling State Park
- Straits State Park
- Tahquamenon Falls State Park
- Tawas Point State Park
- Thompson's Harbor State Park

Silver Lakes State Park

- Traverse City State Park
- Tri-Centennial State Park and Harbor
- Twin Lakes State Park
- Van Buren State Park

- Van Buren Trail State Park
- Van Riper State Park
- Warren Dunes State Park
- Warren Woods State Park
- Wells State Park
- White Pine Trail State Park
- Wilderness State Park
- Wilson State Park
- Young State Park

Recreation areas

- Bald Mountain Recreation Area
- Bass River Recreation Area
- Bay City Recreation Area
- Brighton Recreation Area
- Fort Custer Recreation Area
- Highland Recreation Area
- Holly Recreation Area
- Ionia State Recreation Area
- Island Lake Recreation Area
- Lake Hudson Recreation Area
- Metamora-Hadley Recreation Area
- Ortonville Recreation Area
- Pinckney Recreation Area
- Pontiac Lake Recreation Area
- Proud Lake State Recreation Area
- Rifle River Recreation Area

Proud Lake Recreation Area

- Waterloo Recreation Area
- Wetzel State Recreation Area
- Yankee Springs Recreation Area

State forests

- Au Sable State Forest
- Copper Country State Forest
- Escanaba River State Forest
- Lake Superior State Forest
- Mackinaw State Forest
- Pere Marquette State Forest

The Au Sable River runs through the Au Sable State Forest

Other sites

- Agate Falls Scenic Site
- Bond Falls Scenic Site
- Father Marquette National Memorial - a National Memorial under state supervision
- Laughing Whitefish Falls Scenic Site
- Ralph A. MacMullan Conference Center
- Sturgeon Point Scenic Site
- Wagner Falls Scenic Site

Wagner Falls

External links

- Michigan Department of Natural Resources [1]
- Map of Michigan State Parks [2]

List of National Historic Landmarks in Michigan

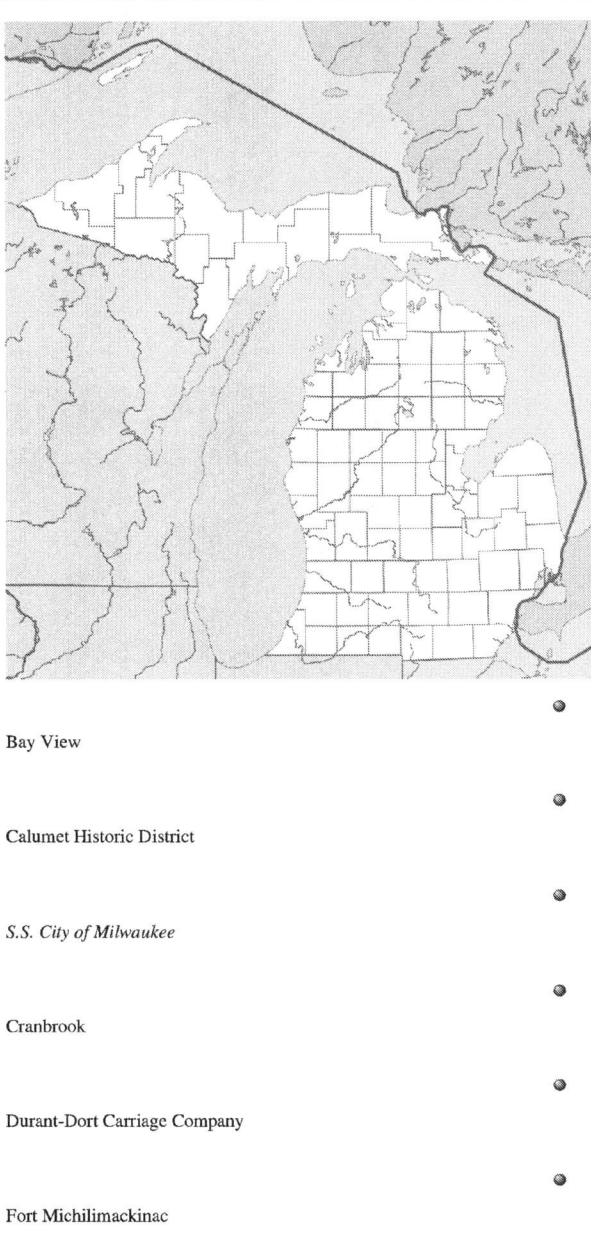

Bay View

Calumet Historic District

S.S. City of Milwaukee

Cranbrook

Durant-Dort Carriage Company

Fort Michilimackinac

List of National Historic Landmarks in Michigan

Grand Hotel
Mackinac Island

Hemingway Cottage

Highland Ford Plant

Lightship No.103
St. Clair Tunnel

Marshall Historic District

State Capitol

Milwaukee Clipper
USS Silversides

Manitou Lifesaving Station

Norton Mounds

Quincy Mining Company

St. Ignace Mission

St. Mary's Falls Canal

Alden Dow House
Herbert H. Dow House

DETROIT

DETROIT NHLs:

Fisher Building

Columbia (Excursion Steamer)

Ford Piquette Ave. Plant

Fox Theater

General Motors Building

Guardian Building

Parke- Davis Laboratory

Pewabic Pottery

Edison Institute

Fair Lane

Ford River Rouge Complex

Michigan National Historic Landmarks (clickable map)

This is a complete **List of National Historic Landmarks in Michigan**, of which there are 34. The United States National Historic Landmark program is operated under the auspices of the National Park Service, and recognizes structures, districts, objects, and similar resources according to a list of criteria of national significance. The state of Michigan is home to 34 of these landmarks.

The table below lists all 34 of these sites, along with added detail and description.

In addition, two sites in Michigan were designated National Historic Landmarks, and subsequently de-designated. One other landmark, a movable object, has been relocated to another state. These three sites appear in another table further below.

Current NHLs in Michigan

List of National Historic Landmarks in Michigan

	Landmark name	Image	Date of designation	Location	County	Description
1	Bay View		1987	Petoskey 45°23′08″N 84°55′49″W	Emmet	Established in 1876 as a Methodist camp meeting, this romantically-planned campground was converted to an independent chautauqua in 1885, a role it served until 1915. These two uniquely American community forms are exemplified in this extensive and well-preserved complex.
2	Calumet Historic District		1989	Calumet 47°14′45″N 88°27′14″W	Houghton	
3	*CITY OF MILWAUKEE* (Great Lakes Car Ferry)		1990	Manistee 44°15′34″N 86°18′58″W	Manistee	
4	*COLUMBIA* (Steamer)		1992	Detroit 42°19′29″N 83°02′38″W	Wayne	
5	Cranbrook		1989	Bloomfield Hills 42°34′23″N 83°14′57″W	Oakland	
6	Alden Dow House and Studio		1989	Midland 43°37′22″N 84°15′18″W	Midland	This house and studio were the residence and acknowledged masterpiece of 20th century architect Alden B. Dow. The quality and originality of his work, as well as his association with Frank Lloyd Wright, have earned him lasting national recognition.
7	Herbert H. Dow House		1976	Midland 43°37′08″N 84°15′10″W	Midland	A home of Herbert H. Dow
8	Durant-Dort Carriage Company Office		1978	Flint 43°01′03″N 83°41′43″W	Genesee	
9	Edison Institute (Greenfield Village and Henry Ford Museum)		1981	Dearborn 42°18′17″N 83°13′55″W	Wayne	

List of National Historic Landmarks in Michigan

10	Fair Lane		1966k	Dearborn 42°18′51″N 83°13′57″W	Wayne	
11	Fisher Building		1989	Detroit 42°22′15″N 83°04′38″W	Wayne	Built in 1927 by the Fisher brothers, this skyscraper is one of the greatest works by architect Albert Kahn. The Fishers spent lavishly to make this Art Deco masterpiece a monumental gift to Detroit and one of the most finely detailed major commercial buildings in the United States.
12	Ford Piquette Avenue Plant		2006	Detroit 42°22′7″N 83°3′55″W	Wayne	
13	Ford River Rouge Complex		1978	Dearborn 42°18′34″N 83°09′44″W	Wayne	
14	Fort Michilimackinac		1960	Mackinaw City 45°47′11″N 84°44′8″W	Emmet	
15	Fox Theater (Detroit)		1989	Detroit 42°20′16″N 83°03′05″W	Wayne	
16	General Motors Building		1978	Detroit 42°22′09″N 83°04′32″W	Wayne	
17	Grand Hotel		1989	Mackinac Island 45°50′56″N 84°37′33″W	Mackinac	
18	Guardian Building		1989	Detroit 42°19′45″N 83°02′46″W	Wayne	
19	Ernest Hemingway Cottage		1968	Walloon Lake 45°16′41″N 84°59′58″W	Emmet	Boyhood summer home of author Ernest Hemingway. His father built the house in 1900 when his son was a year old, and it was here the future writer learned to hunt and fish and appreciate the outdoor life he came to celebrate in his writings.

20	Highland Park Ford Plant		1978	Highland Park 42°24′38″N 83°06′02″W	Wayne	
21	LIGHTSHIP NO. 103 "*HURON*"		December 20, 1989	Port Huron 42°59′15″N 82°25′36″W	St. Clair	
22	Mackinac Island		1960	Mackinac Island 45°52′N 84°38′W	Mackinac	This island's key role in the early fur trade was secured by its location at the center of the Great Lakes region. Hosting the northern headquarters of John Jacob Astor's American Fur Company until the 1840s, it preserves numerous buildings relating to the fur industry. Its geopolitical importance is illustrated at Fort Mackinac; control of this strategic island was not settled until the 1814 Treaty of Ghent.
23	Marshall Historic District		1991	Marshall 42°16′19″N 84°57′51″W	Calhoun	
24	Michigan State Capitol		1992	Lansing 42°44′01″N 84°33′14″W	Ingham	
25	*MILWAUKEE CLIPPER* (Passenger Steamship)		1989	Muskegon	Muskegon	
26	North Manitou Island Lifesaving Station		1998	Sleeping Bear Dunes National Lakeshore 45°07′09″N 85°58′39″W	Leelanau	
27	Norton Mound Group		1965	Grand Rapids	Kent	Center of Hopewellian culture in the western Great Lakes region, from ca. 400 B.C. to A.D. 400.

List of National Historic Landmarks in Michigan

28	Parke-Davis Research Laboratory		1976	Detroit 42°20′06″N 83°00′52″W	Wayne	Built in 1902, this was the first industrial research laboratory in the U.S. established for the specific purpose of conducting pharmacological research, inaugurating the commercial pure science approach which has driven the rapid development of pharmaceutical technology. National Park Service staff recommended withdrawal of landmark status in 2002 due to loss of the building's historic integrity during conversion to a hotel.
29	Pewabic Pottery		1991	Detroit 42°21′42″N 82°58′52″W	Wayne	This 1907 building, designed by William Stratton, is the home of ceramic artist Mary Chase Perry Stratton's studio and production facilities. Her work in the Arts and Crafts movement raised the artistic standard of American pottery, and is featured architecturally or curatorially in numerous prominent buildings and distinguished institutions.
30	Quincy Mining Company Historic District		1989	Hancock 47°8′7″N 88°34′33″W	Houghton	
31	St. Clair River Tunnel		1993	Port Huron 42°57′29″N 82°25′59″W	St. Clair	
32	St. Ignace Mission		1960	St. Ignace 45°52′11″N 84°44′38″W	Mackinac	Now a park, this was the site of a mission established by Père Jacques Marquette, and the site of his grave in 1677. A second mission was established at a different site in 1837, and moved here in 1954.
33	St. Mary's Falls Canal		1966	Sault Ste. Marie 46°30′11″N 84°21′17″W	Chippewa	
34	*USS SILVERSIDES* (Submarine)		1986	Muskegon	Muskegon	

Former NHLs in Michigan

Landmark name	Image	Year listed	Locality	County	Description
Lincoln Motor Company Plant		1978, withdrawn 2005	Detroit	Wayne	Henry M. Leland acquired a factory here in 1917 and greatly expanded it in order to produce Liberty Engines as part of the World War I war effort. After the war, Leland used his long and prominent experience with Cadillac to inaugurate the Lincoln line of automobiles. Leland sold his company to Henry Ford in 1922; by 1952 this original Lincoln plant was retired from automotive production. Most of the complex was demolished in 2002/03, leading to withdrawal of its landmark designation.
Reo Motor Car Company Plant		1978, withdrawn 1985	Lansing	Ingham	In his third venture in the automotive industry, and after his departure from the highly successful Oldsmobile, Ransom E. Olds established the Reo Motor Car Company at this plant in 1904. Reo enjoyed early success and was responsible for many innovations in automobile manufacturing, but remained a niche company for most of its existence. The factory complex was demolished in 1980 to make way for site redevelopment, and landmark status was withdrawn in 1985.
Ste. Claire (passenger steamboat)		1992	Ecorse (formerly)	Wayne (formerly)	Relocated to Ohio.

See also

- List of Registered Historic Places in Michigan
- List of U.S. National Historic Landmarks by state
- Detroit Historical Museum
- Historic preservation
- History of Michigan
- Michigan Department of History, Arts and Libraries
- Michigan History magazine
- National Register of Historic Places

External links

- National Historic Landmark Program [1] at the National Park Service
- Lists of National Historic Landmarks [2]

Overview of Saginaw

Saginaw, Michigan

Saginaw	
— City —	

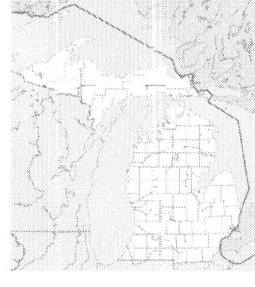 Saginaw Location of Saginaw within Saginaw County, Michigan	
Coordinates: 43°25′10″N 83°56′58″W	
Country	United States
State	Michigan
County	Saginaw
Settled	1819
Incorporated	1857

Government	
- Type	Council-Manager
- Mayor	Greg Branch
- City Manager	Darnell Earley
Area	
- City	18.2 sq mi (47.1 km^2)
- Land	17.4 sq mi (45.2 km^2)
- Water	0.7 sq mi (1.9 km^2)
Elevation	584 ft (178 m)
Population (2000)	
- City	61799
- Estimate (2009)	55238
- Density	3542.9/sq mi (1367/km^2)
- Urban	140985
- Metro	206300
Time zone	EST (UTC-5)
- Summer (DST)	EDT (UTC-4)
ZIP Code	48601, 48602, 48605, 48607
Area code(s)	989
FIPS code	26-70520
GNIS feature ID	1627020
Website	http://www.saginaw-mi.com

Saginaw is a city in the U.S. state of Michigan and the seat of Saginaw County. The city of Saginaw was once a thriving lumber town and manufacturing center. Saginaw and Saginaw County lie in the Flint/Tri-Cities region of Michigan. It is located adjacent to Saginaw Charter Township and considered part of the Tri-Cities area, along with Bay City and Midland. As of the 2000 census, the city had a total population of 61,799. In 2009, the U.S. Census Bureau estimated its population to be 55,238.

History

Main article: History of Saginaw, Michigan

The site of what is presently the city of Saginaw was originally inhabited by Native Americans. The Sauk lived in the area and were driven from the area by Ojibwe (Chippewa). The name Saginaw is believed to mean "where the Sauk were" in the Ojibwe language. French missionaries and traders first appeared in the area during the late 17th century. The first permanent settlement by those other than Native Americans was in 1815 when Louis Campau established a trading post on the west bank of the Saginaw River. Shortly thereafter the United States established Fort Saginaw.

During Michigan's territorial period, a county and township government were organized at Saginaw. Growth of the settlement was fueled rapidly during the 19th century by the lumber industry. Saginaw was the site of numerous sawmills and served as a port for Great Lakes vessels. What is now the city of Saginaw resulted from the consolidation of the cities of East Saginaw and Saginaw (West Side) in 1889.

During the 20th century, Saginaw's economy was dominated by manufacturing related to the automotive industry. Immigration from other areas, particularly the American south, swelled the population. This population growth particularly expanded the presence of African-Americans in Saginaw. The politics of the city became dominated with issues of race relations. The manufacturing presence in Saginaw declined in the latter half of the 20th century and the population diminished as well. Saginaw has faced increasing social problems relating to poverty as a result of its high rate of unemployment. Crime has been a major area of concern for the community in recent years.

Geography

Topography

According to the United States Census Bureau, the city has a total area of 18.2 square miles (47.1 km²), of which, 17.4 square miles (45.2 km²) of it is land and 0.7 square miles (1.9 km²) of it (3.96%) is water. Saginaw lies on the Saginaw River, 15 miles (24 km) inland from the Saginaw Bay, an arm of Lake Huron.

Climate

Climate data for Saginaw, Michigan													
Month	Jan	Feb	Mar	Apr	May	Jun	Jul	Aug	Sep	Oct	Nov	Dec	Year
Average high °F (°C)	32 (0)	33 (0.6)	38 (3.3)	53 (11.7)	67 (19.4)	79 (26.1)	82 (27.8)	80 (26.7)	71 (21.7)	62 (16.7)	44 (6.7)	34 (1.1)	56 (13.3)
Average low °F (°C)	18 (-7.8)	19 (-7.2)	23 (-5)	33 (0.6)	44 (6.7)	56 (13.3)	59 (15)	56 (13.3)	48 (8.9)	40 (4.4)	29 (-1.7)	21 (-6.1)	37 (2.8)
Precipitation inches (mm)	2.2 (56)	2.2 (56)	2.3 (58)	3.2 (81)	1.8 (46)	3.2 (81)	3.6 (91)	2.5 (64)	3.4 (86)	3.2 (81)	2.4 (61)	2.5 (64)	32.5 (826)
Source: Weatherbase													

Demographics

Saginaw is the largest principal city of the Saginaw-Bay City-Saginaw Township North CSA, a Combined Statistical Area that includes the Saginaw-Saginaw Township North (Saginaw County) and Bay City (Bay County) metropolitan areas, which had a combined population of 320,196 at the 2000 census.

As of the census of 2000, there were 61,799 people, 23,182 households, and 15,114 families residing in the city. The population density was 3,542.9 people per square mile (1,368.2/km²). There were 25,639 housing units at an average density of 1,469.9/sq mi (567.6/km²). The racial makeup of the city was 47.02% White, 43.26% African American, 0.49% Native American, 0.33% Asian, 0.02% Pacific Islander, 5.86% from other races, and 3.03% from two or more races. Hispanic or Latino of any race were 11.75% of the population.

Location of the Saginaw-Bay City-Saginaw Township North CSA and its components: Saginaw-Saginaw Township North Metropolitan Statistical Area   Bay City Metropolitan Statistical Area

There were 23,182 households out of which 35.4% had children under the age of 18 living with them, 32.9% were married couples living together, 27.3% had a female householder with no husband present, and 34.8% were non-families. 29.5% of all households were made up of individuals and 9.9% had someone living alone who was 65 years of age or older. The average household size was 2.60 and the average family size was 3.23.

In the city the population was spread out with 31.6% under the age of 18, 9.9% from 18 to 24, 28.3% from 25 to 44, 18.7% from 45 to 64, and 11.4% who were 65 years of age or older. The median age was 31 years. For every 100 females there were 87.2 males. For every 100 females age 18 and over, there were 81.0 males.

The median income for a household in the city was $26,485, and the median income for a family was $29,945. Males had a median income of $31,614 versus $22,714 for females. The per capita income for the city was $13,816. About 24.7% of families and 28.5% of the population were below the poverty line, including 40.2% of those under age 18 and 16.3% of those age 65 or over.

Law and government

Government

Main article: Government of Saginaw, Michigan

Saginaw is classified as a Home Rule City under the Michigan Home Rule Cities Act which permits cities to exercise "Home Rule" powers, among which is the power to frame and adopt its own City Charter which serves as the fundamental law of the city, in a manner similar to a Constitution for a national or state government. The present Charter was adopted in 1935 and took effect on January 6, 1936. Pursuant to the City Charter, Saginaw is governed by a nine member elected at-large Council. The term of office for a member of the City Council is four years commencing with the first meeting following a regular municipal election. The terms of Council members are staggered so that the entire Council is not subject to re-election at the same time; alternatively either four or five members are elected in each odd-numbered year.

Crime

According to Federal Bureau of Investigation statistics Saginaw has ranked as the number one most violent city in America from 2003 through September 2010 when the most recent statistics were released. The ranking is based on violent crimes per person for cities with populations greater than 40,000. Included in the definition of violent crimes are murder, non-negligent manslaughter, forcible rape, robbery and aggravated assault.

Education

Higher education

The City of Saginaw is served by Delta College and Saginaw Valley State University, which are located in nearby University Center, Michigan and a campus of Davenport University, located in Kochville Township. Central Michigan University maintains an off-campus center inside the city that offers numerous degree programs.

Primary and secondary schools

See also: List of schools in Saginaw, Michigan

The City of Saginaw is served by the Saginaw Public School District (SPSD). The district operates 14 elementary schools, 2 combined elementary/middle schools; Arthur Eddy Academy K-8, and Zilwaukee K-8, 2 middle schools; Reuben Daniels Middle School and Willie E. Thompson Middle School, and 4 high schools. The district is governed by a seven member elected board of education. The board selects a superintendent for the district. The current superintendent is Dr. Carlton Jenkins. The three public high schools in Saginaw are Arthur Hill High School, Saginaw High School, and the Saginaw Arts and Sciences Academy. Michigan Lutheran Seminary is the lone private high school in the city. Charter schools in the city are North Saginaw Charter Academy and Saginaw Prep schools.

Infrastructure

Utilities

The City of Saginaw gets its electricity and natural gas from Consumers Energy.

Municipal water supply

In 1929, the city opened its consolidated water works plant which replaced two separate plants that were on each side of the Saginaw river. This plant treated water brought in from the Saginaw river and piped it out to the residents as well as corner pumps for people that did not have direct connections to the system. Currently, the City of Saginaw jointly owns with the City of Midland the Saginaw-Midland Municipal Water Supply Corporation. Incorporated in 1946, this water treatment system has supplied drinking and industrial water to both cities and many surrounding areas within the county. Due to brackish water being in the aquifers below both cities, a 65-mile (105 km) long pipeline was constructed in 1948 to supply water from Lake Huron at White Stone Point, north of Au Gres to water treatment plants in Saginaw and Midland with a second pipe added by 1996. This system has played a role in the decline of the city. The City of Saginaw, in order to obtain new sources of revenue, sold water to areas outside of the city (especially to the Saginaw Charter Township). This caused numerous businesses inside the city to leave for the surrounding areas and development in the city to stagnate.

The City of Midland, however, adopted a policy of "No Annexation, No Water" which has led to the growth of the city as well as the surrounding areas.

Neighborhoods

Despite its size, The City of Saginaw consists of many neighborhoods, including:

- Downtown
- Old Town
- Southwest Village
- Northmoor
- Heritage Square
- Cathedral District
- Houghton Jones Neighborhood
- South East Side
- Triangle Parks
- St. Stephen's Area
- Brockway-Carmen Park
- Butman-Fish Neighborhood
- Redeemer Area
- Saginaw High Neighborhood
- Northeast Side
- Covenant Neighborhood
- The Sandhill
- The Woods

Transportation

Saginaw is served primarily by two airports; MBS International Airport, located in nearby Freeland, and Bishop International Airport, located in Flint. Saginaw is also served by three smaller airports; Harry W. Browne Airport in adjacent Buena Vista Township, James Clements Municipal Airport in Bay City, and Jack Barstow Municipal Airport in Midland. In addition to the airports, Interstate 75 serves as the main arterial route for the Saginaw area while Interstate 675 provides direct access to the center of the city from Interstate 75. Interstate 69 is a nearby east-west corridor providing access to the rest of the Midwestern United States and Canada. The Saginaw River runs through the middle of the city and provides access to Saginaw Bay and the rest of the Great Lakes via docks on the northern side of the city. Historically, ships were able to move all along the length of the river inside the city but fixed bridges being built over the river closed access south of the northern docks. In the city and surrounding areas, mass transit is provided by bus under the authority of the Saginaw Transit Authority Regional Services (STARS) system. The STARS system connects to Bay City's Bus system at Saginaw

Valley State University.

Major highways

![I-75]	I-75 passes along the eastern side of the city through Buena Vista Charter Township.
![I-675]	I-675 provides a short freeway loop through downtown Saginaw and back to I-75 through Saginaw Charter Township.
![M-13]	M-13 runs from I-69 through downtown Saginaw and north to Standish.
![M-46]	M-46 is a cross-peninsular road, running across the mitten and the thumb – from Port Sanilac on the Lake Huron shore, through Saginaw, and then on to Muskegon on the Lake Michigan shore. This east-west surface route nearly bisects the Lower Peninsula of Michigan latitudinally.
![M-47]	M-47 passes through the western suburbs and provides a direct connection to MBS International Airport.
![M-52]	M-52 runs from the Ohio border through Adrian and Owosso before ending at M-46, in the western suburbs of Saginaw. M-52 also provides an alternate connection to Lansing, Michigan's state capitol.
![M-58]	M-58 runs from M-47 to I-675.
![M-81]	M-81 runs east from M-13 to Caro and Cass City and ends at M-53 in Sanilac County.
![M-84]	M-84 runs from downtown Bay City to M-58 in Saginaw.

Culture and entertainment

The city's main entertainment can be found in the downtown area, where places such as the Children's Zoo, The Dow Event Center and the restored Temple Theatre offer live entertainment. The Dow Event Center is also home to the city's junior ice hockey team, the Saginaw Spirit of the Ontario Hockey League as well as The Saginaw Sting, an indoor football team. The downtown area, which contains a number of office buildings from the late 19th century and early 20th century, is located near the Saginaw Club, a local businessmen's club founded in 1889, and the Saginaw Center, an educational complex run by Delta College. Once vibrant, the downtown area has been in decline in recent years and presently struggles with blight. Downtown is not to be confused with the Old Town/West Side City area located on the other side of the river and about one mile (1.6 km) south. Old Town houses many popular bars, locally owned restaurants, and arts organizations.

Castle Museum (Saginaw) is on the National Register of Historic Places.

Sports

The Saginaw area is home to two professional sports teams as well as one NCAA Division-II school that has various sports programs. The Saginaw Spirit is an Ontario Hockey League team that became nationally known when television personality Stephen Colbert promoted the team on his show, *The Colbert Report*. The Saginaw Sting is an indoor football team that formed in 2007 to play in Saginaw beginning in the 2008 season. At the collegiate level, Saginaw Valley State University competes in numerous sports such as American Football, Basketball, and Volleyball.

Team	Sport	League	Year founded	Venue
Saginaw Spirit	Ice hockey	Ontario Hockey League	2002	Dow Event Center
Saginaw Sting	Indoor football	Continental Indoor Football League	2008	Dow Event Center
Saginaw Valley State University	Various	Great Lakes Intercollegiate Athletic Conference	1963	SVSU Campus

Shopping Areas

The area's main shopping district is located along Bay Rd. and Tittabawassee Road north of town, where several big box stores can be found. Also in the same area is Fashion Square Mall, a regional shopping mall anchored by JCPenney, Macy's, and Sears. There are also many restaurants in this part of town, primarily regional chains. Out-lying shopping exists for Saginaw Township residents along State Street, which is a main corridor through the township district. There are smaller businesses, consisting mostly of grocery stores, convenience stores, gas stations and other service style businesses.

Media

Television stations

Saginaw is part of Nielsen's Flint-Saginaw-Bay City-Midland Designated Market Area which is the 66th largest market in the United States for Television Viewers. Saginaw is the home of CBS affiliate WNEM which maintains its studios and offices inside the City though its license is for Bay City, MI. ABC affiliate WJRT maintains its offices and newsrooms in Saginaw while its studios are in its community of license, Flint. Only NBC affiliate WEYI and Christian station WAQP have the City of Saginaw as their city of record but both maintain their facilities outside of the city. Charter Communications operates a cable television network servicing the City of Saginaw under a franchise agreement.

Saginaw, Michigan

Television stations in the Saginaw, Michigan area (*Ascending order*)			
Channel	Call letters	Description	Comments
5	WNEM-TV	CBS affiliate	Licensed to Bay City; studios in Saginaw
12	WJRT-TV	ABC O&O affiliate	Based and licensed in Flint
19	WDCQ-TV	PBS member station	Licensed to Bad Axe; studios at Delta College in University Center
25	WEYI-TV	NBC affiliate	Licensed to Saginaw; studios in Clio
42	W46CR	3ABN affiliate	Based and licensed in Saginaw
46	WBSF	CW affiliate	Licensed to Bay City; studios in Clio
49	WAQP	TCT O&O affiliate	Based and licensed in Saginaw
66	WSMH	Fox affiliate	Based and licensed in Flint

Radio stations

Radio stations licensed within the immediate Saginaw area (Saginaw County) are listed. Many locations in the City of Saginaw also receive stations from Bay City, Midland, Flint, and Lansing.

AM radio stations					
Frequency	Call sign	Name	Format	Owner	City
790 AM	WSGW	Newsradio 790	News/Talk	NextMedia Group	Saginaw, Michigan
1250 AM	WNEM	WNEM 1250 AM	News/Talk	Meredith Corporation	Saginaw, Michigan
1400 AM	WSAM	The Bay	Soft adult contemporary	MacDonald Broadcasting	Saginaw, Michigan

FM radio stations					
Frequency	Call sign	Name	Format	Owner	City
90.9 FM	WTRK	Air 1	Contemporary Christian	Educational Media Foundation	Saginaw, Michigan
93.3 FM	WKQZ	The Rock Station, Z93	Modern rock	Citadel Broadcasting	Saginaw, Michigan
93.7 FM	WRCL	Club 93.7	Rhythmic contemporary	Regent Communications	Saginaw, Michigan
94.5 FM	WCEN	94.5 The Moose	Country music	NextMedia Group	Saginaw, Michigan
96.1 FM	WHNN	Oldies 96	Oldies	Citadel Broadcasting	Saginaw, Michigan
97.3 FM	WMJO	97.3 Joe FM	Classic hits/Hot AC	MacDonald Broadcasting	Saginaw, Michigan
98.1 FM	WKCQ	98FM KCQ	Country music	MacDonald Broadcasting	Saginaw, Michigan

100.5 FM	WTKQ	FM Talk 100.5	News/Talk	NextMedia Group	Saginaw, Michigan
102.5 FM	WIOG	The Hit Music Channel	Contemporary hits	Citadel Broadcasting	Saginaw, Michigan
104.1 FM	WSAM	The Bay	Soft adult contemporary	MacDonald Broadcasting	Bridgeport, Michigan
104.5 FM	WILZ	Wheelz 104.5	Classic rock	Citadel Broadcasting	Saginaw, Michigan
106.3 FM	WGER	The New Mix 106.3	Adult contemporary music	NextMedia Group	Saginaw, Michigan
107.1 FM	WTLZ	KISS 107.1	Urban adult contemporary	NextMedia Group	Saginaw, Michigan

Newspapers

- *The Saginaw News* — Thursday, Friday, Sunday
- *Review Magazine* [1] — biweekly
- *The Saginaw Press* — weekly

Museums and gardens

The Andersen Enrichment Center and Lucille E. Andersen Memorial Rose Garden are part of the Saginaw's park system. These locations are used to host private and public events throughout the year. Past events have included, Hollyday Art Fair and a World AIDS Day service The garden includes a fountain with a sculpture by Marshall Fredericks.

The Saginaw Art Museum hosts temporary exhibitions and permanent collections. The museum also houses The John and Michele Bueker Research Library and Archives of Michigan Art. The museum originated as the home of C.L. Ring who commissioned Charles A. Platt to design the house and gardens. The museum opened to the public in 1948. The museum is a Smithsonian Institution affiliate.

When it comes to the historical aspects of Saginaw, no place shows it off as well as the Castle Museum of Saginaw County History. The museum is housed in a former post office which was built to resemble a castle, and honors the French heritage of the area. With over 100,000 artifacts in their collection, the Historical Society of Saginaw County displays items from their collection as well as traveling exhibits.

Saginaw in popular culture and literature

- Saginaw is referred to in the Simon & Garfunkel song "America", which is about hitchhiking across the USA. It was noted: "It took me four days to hitchhike from Saginaw, I've gone to look for America."
- Bill Anderson and Don Wayne wrote a song entitled "Saginaw, Michigan" that has been covered by a dozen artists. Cowboy singer Lefty Frizzell was the first to perform it, with his version reaching number one on the country charts. Also popularly, it was performed by Johnny Cash. The song mis-situates the city on Saginaw Bay, about 15 miles to the north.
- Saginaw was also referred to as "dreadful" by the bold character Miss Ferenczi in the short story "Gryphon" by Charles Baxter.
- Saginaw served as the destination point for the Seinfeld characters Kramer and Newman during an episode where the pair hatched a scheme to transport bottles and cans via a United States Postal Service mail truck from New York to Michigan to earn 10¢ per recycled item, as opposed to New York's 5¢.

Notable natives

Main article: List of people from Saginaw, Michigan

See also: Category:People from Saginaw, Michigan

Sister cities

- ● Tokushima, Japan
- Zapopan, Jalisco, Mexico
- Awka, Anambra, Nigeria

See also

- Saginaw Trail

External links

- City of Saginaw [2]
- Saginaw County Chamber of Commerce [3]
- *Saginaw News* [4]
- Saginaw Club [5]
- Saginaw Jaycees [6]
- Saginaw Valley Amateur Radio Association [7]
- Saginaw county citizen corps [8]

- Old Town Saginaw Music Association (CTSMA) [9]
- Historical Society of Saginaw County [10]
- Saginaw Art Museum [11]
- Saginaw Valley State University [12]
- Marshall Fredericks Sculpture Museum [13]
- Saginaw Railway Museum [14]

Saginaw County, Michigan

Saginaw County, Michigan	
Seal	
Location in the state of Michigan	
Michigan's location in the U.S.	
Founded	February 9, 1835 [1]
Seat	Saginaw
Area - Total - Land - Water	816 sq mi (2113 km²) 809 sq mi (2095 km²) 7 sq mi (18 km²), 0.84%
Population - (2000) - Density	210039 259/sq mi (100/km²)
Website	www.saginawcounty.com [2]

Saginaw County is a county in the U.S. state of Michigan. As of the 2000 census, the population was 210,039 with the 2009 Census Bureau estimate placing the population at 200,050, making it the 10th most populated county in Michigan. The county seat is Saginaw. The county was created by September 10, 1822, and was fully organized on February 9, 1835. *Saginaw* is a Native American term, perhaps having reference to the Sauk tribe who lived at the mouth of the river. Another source opines that: "There are two possible derivations: from 'Sace-nong' or 'Sak-e-nong' (Sauk Town) because the Sauk (Sac) once lived there, or from Chippewa words meaning 'place of the outlet' from 'sag' (an opening) and 'ong' (place of)." *See* List of Michigan county name etymologies.

Geography

- According to the U.S. Census Bureau, the county has a total area of 816 square miles (2,113 km²), of which, 809 square miles (2,095 km²) of it is land and 7 square miles (18 km²) of it (0.84%) is water.
- The Roman Catholic Diocese of Saginaw is the controlling regional body for the Catholic Church.
- Saginaw is considered to be part of Flint/Tri-Cities.

Geographic features

The County has no natural lakes, but many rivers. The Saginaw River is the waterway that completes the Saginaw River Watershed, which is the largest watershed in the State of Michigan. Other rivers that source the Saginaw include Cass, Flint, Shiawassee, Bad, and Tittabawassee.

- Cass River has many branches, one of which flows into the Shiawassee River in the Shiawassee National Wildlife Refuge at 43°22′42″N 83°59′04″W less than a mile from where the Shiawassee merges with the Tittabawassee River to form the Saginaw River. The Refuge is entirely within Saginaw County.

Airports

Scheduled airline service is available from MBS International Airport near Freeland, Michigan and Bishop International Airport in Flint, Michigan.. Harry Browne Airport in Buena Vista Charter Township also serves the region.

Interstates

- I-75
- I-675

Saginaw County, Michigan

US Highways

- [23] US-23

Michigan State Trunklines

- [13] M-13 runs from I-69 through downtown Saginaw and north to Standish.
- [15] M-15
- [46] M-46 is a cross peninsular road, running across the mitten and the thumb—from Port Sanilac on the Lake Huron shore; through Saginaw near Saginaw Bay; and then on to Muskegon on the Lake Michigan shore. This east-west surface route nearly bisects the Lower Peninsula of Michigan latitudinally.
- [47] M-47 passes through the western suburbs and provides a direct connection to MBS International Airport in Freeland before ending at US 10 in nearby Bay County.
- [52] M-52 runs from the Ohio border through Adrian and Owosso before ending at M-46, in the western suburbs of Saginaw. M-52 also provides an alternate connection to Lansing, Michigan's state capitol.
- [54] M-54
- [57] M-57
- [58] M-58 runs from M-47 to I-675.
- [81] M-81 runs east from M-13 to Caro and Cass City and ends at M-53 in Sanilac County.
- [83] M-83
- [84] M-84 runs from downtown Bay City to M-58 in Saginaw.

Adjacent counties

- Bay County (northeast)
- Midland County (northwest)
- Tuscola County (east)
- Gratiot County (west)
- Genesee County (southeast)
- Shiawassee County (south)
- Clinton County (southwest)

National protected area

- Shiawassee National Wildlife Refuge

Demographics

As of the census of 2000, there were 210,039 people, 80,430 households, and 55,818 families residing in the county. The population density was 260 people per square mile (100/km²). There were 85,505 housing units at an average density of 106 per square mile (41/km²). The racial makeup of the county was 75.33% White, 18.62% Black or African American, 0.41% Native American, 0.80% Asian, 0.01% Pacific Islander, 2.88% from other races, and 1.95% from two or more races. 6.70% of the population were Hispanic or Latino of any race. 27.4% were of German, 7.2% Polish, 5.9% English, 5.6% Irish and 5.4% American ancestry according to Census 2000. 93.9% spoke English and 3.7% Spanish as their first language.

There were 80,430 households out of which 32.70% had children under the age of 18 living with them, 50.20% were married couples living together, 15.40% had a female householder with no husband present, and 30.60% were non-families. 26.00% of all households were made up of individuals and 10.40% had someone living alone who was 65 years of age or older. The average household size was 2.54 and the average family size was 3.06.

In the county the population was spread out with 26.60% under the age of 18, 9.00% from 18 to 24, 27.60% from 25 to 44, 23.20% from 45 to 64, and 13.50% who were 65 years of age or older. The median age was 36 years. For every 100 females there were 92.50 males. For every 100 females age 18 and over, there were 88.40 males.

The median income for a household in the county was $38,637, and the median income for a family was $46,494. Males had a median income of $40,514 versus $25,419 for females. The per capita income for the county was $19,438. About 11.00% of families and 13.90% of the population were below the poverty line, including 20.70% of those under age 18 and 9.50% of those age 65 or over.

Government and politics

The county government operates the jail, maintains rural roads, operates the major local courts, keeps files of deeds and mortgages, maintains vital records, administers public health regulations, and participates with the state in the provision of welfare and other social services. The county board of commissioners controls the budget but has only limited authority to make laws or ordinances. In Michigan, most local government functions — police and fire, building and zoning, tax assessment, street maintenance, etc. — are the responsibility of individual cities and townships.

Saginaw County elected officials

- Prosecuting Attorney: Michael D. Thomas
- Sheriff: William Federspiel
- County Clerk: Susan Kaltenbach
- County Treasurer: Marvin D. Hare
- Register of Deeds: Mildred M. Dodak
- Public Works Commissioner: James A. Koski

All countywide officers are elected for four-year terms. The next scheduled election for these offices is November of 2012.

(information as of June 2010)

Cities, villages, and townships

Cities

- City of Frankenmuth - independent of Frankenmuth Township
- City of Saginaw - county seat; most populous political subdivision in the county; independent of Saginaw Charter Township
- City of Zilwaukee - independent of Zilwaukee Township

Villages

Under Michigan law, villages are municipal corporations but are not independent of the townships in which they are located. A village resident also is a resident of a township, is liable for taxes to both units of government and may vote in both village and township elections, if eligible.

- Village of Birch Run - located in Birch Run Township
- Village of Chesaning - located in Chesaning Township
- Village of Merrill - located in Jonesfield Township
- Village of Oakley - located in Brady Township
- Village St. Charles - located mainly in St. Charles Township with portions in Brant Township and Swan Creek Township

Saginaw County, Michigan

Townships

- Albee Township
- Birch Run Township
- Blumfield Township
- Brady Township
- Brant Township
- Bridgeport Charter Township
- Buena Vista Charter Township
- Carrollton Township
- Chapin Township
- Chesaning Township
- Frankenmuth Township - independent of the City of Frankenmuth
- Fremont Township
- James Township
- Jonesfield Township
- Kochville Township
- Lakefield Township
- Maple Grove Township
- Marion Township
- Richland Township
- Saginaw Charter Township - independent of the City of Saginaw
- Spaulding Township
- St. Charles Township
- Swan Creek Township
- Taymouth Township
- Thomas Township
- Tittabawassee Township
- Zilwaukee Township - independent of the City of Zilwaukee

Unincorporated Places

- Bridgeport, CDP
- Buena Vista, CDP
- Burt, CDP
- Freeland, CDP
- Hemlock, CDP
- Robin Glen-Indiantown, CDP
- Shields, CDP
- Alicia
- Blumfield Corners
- Brady Center
- Brant
- Carrollton
- Chapin
- Clausedale
- Crow Island
- Dice
- Fenmore
- Fergus
- Fordney
- Fosters
- Frankentrost
- Frost
- Galloway‡
- Garfield
- Gera
- Groveton
- Indiantown
- Iva
- Kochville
- Lakefield
- Lawndale
- Layton Corners
- Luce
- Marion Springs
- Morseville
- Nelson
- Orr
- Racy
- Raines
- Farshallburg
- Roosevelt
- Shattuckville
- Shields
- Swan Creek
- Taymouth

Notable natives

Main article: List of people from Saginaw, Michigan

See also: Category:People from Saginaw, Michigan\

- Theodore Roethke (1908 - 1963) Pulitzer prize and National Book Award winning poet was born and buried here.

Historical markers

There are twenty eight recognized historical markers in the county: They are:

- Bliss Park
- Burt Opera House / Wellington R. Burt
- Coal Mine No. 8
- The Cushway House / Benjamin Cushway and Adelaide Cushway
- First Congregational Church [Saginaw]
- Fowler Schoolhouse (Fremont Township)
- Frankenmuth / Saint Lorenz Evangelical Lutheran Church
- Frankenmuth Bavarian Inn
- Freeland United Methodist Church
- George Nason House
- Hess School
- Hoyt Library
- Leamington Stewart House
- Michigan's German Settlers
- Morseville Bridge
- Presbyterian Church of South Saginaw
- Saginaw Club
- Saginaw Oil Industry
- Saginaw Post Office
- Saginaw Valley Coal
- Saginaw Valley Lumbering Era
- St. Mary's Hospital
- Saint Michael Catholic Parish
- St. Paul's Episcopal Mission
- Shroeder House
- Theodore Roethke / Childhood Home

See also

- Saginaw Trail

Further reading

- Clarke Historical Library, Central Michigan University, Bibliography for Saginaw County. [3]

External links

- Saginaw County [4]
- [5]

Geographical coordinates: 43°20′N 84°03′W

Flint/Tri-Cities

Flint/Tri-Cities	
Mid Michigan	
Lower Peninsula of Michigan	
Country	United States
State	Michigan
The Flint/Tri-Cities Region is highlighted in red.	

The **Flint/Tri-Cities Region** is a region in the Lower Peninsula of the U.S. state of Michigan. Flint/Tri-Cities has two subregions, **The Thumb** and the **Greater Tri Cities**. Flint's population is 124,943, the fifth largest city in Michigan, the combined population of the Greater Tri-Cities (Saginaw, Midland, and Bay City) is 398,482. Genesee, St. Clair and Lapeer counties are located in Detroit–Ann Arbor–Flint Combined Statistical Area.

Economy

The Flint and Tri-Cities area, as well as most of Michigan is dependent on manufacturing.[*citation needed*] Automobile manufacturing is most prevalent in Saginaw and Flint, whereas Midland is the headquarters of the Dow Chemical Company, the world's second largest chemical producer. Rural areas grow crops such as sugar beets, navy beans, corn, fruits, and fish from the Saginaw Bay and Lake Huron.

Business

Several large corporations have operations in the Tri-Cities. The Michigan Sugar Company, which is a cooperative owned by 1250 farmers, operates factories in Bay City, Caro, Croswell, and Sebewaing. General Motors operates the Flint Truck Assembly factory in Flint and Powertrain plants in Flint, Bay City, and Saginaw. The Dow Chemical Company's world headquarters is based in Midland. Delphi Corporation operates Delphi Saginaw Steering Systems in Saginaw. S.C. Johnson and Son has a manufacturing facility in Bay City making Ziploc products.

Geography

- *See also* List of Michigan state parks and geography of Michigan.

Counties included

- Genesee County, Michigan

The Greater Tri Cities

- Midland County, Michigan
- Bay County, Michigan
- Saginaw County, Michigan

The Thumb

- Huron County, Michigan
- Tuscola County, Michigan
- Sanilac County, Michigan
- Lapeer County, Michigan
- St. Clair County, Michigan

Geographic features

The area has many lakes and rivers.

- Cass River has many branches, one of which flows into the Shiawassee River in the Shiawassee National Wildlife Refuge at 43°22′42″N 83°59′04″W less than a mile from where the Shiawassee merges with the Tittabawassee River to form the Saginaw River
- The Saginaw Bay forms a low basin known as the Saginaw Valley, which covers most of the region.
- Lake Huron rests in the far eastern portion of the area, known as the thumb
- St. Clair River, connects Lake Huron to Lake St. Clair, and is the farthest east border in Michigan. It forms a low impression in eastern St. Clair County, and has a delta at its mouth (North America's largest freshwater delta), which includes Harsens Island and Walpole Island, Ontario. Ferries cross the river at Algonac and Marine City, these being international border crossings.
- Flint River Flows through the central and southern portion of Lapeer County, west into Genesee County, and then merges into the Saginaw River.

Flint/Tri-Cities

Transportation

Airlines and airports

Scheduled airline service is available from MBS International Airport near Midland, Michigan and Flint Bishop International Airport. The only international airport in the thumb area is St. Clair County International Airport about 6 miles outside Port Huron.

Highways

Interstate highways

- Interstate 69 cuts through the southern area of the region. It starts at the Blue Water Bridge in Port Huron, and runs through Flint.
- Interstate 75 connects this region together. It runs through Bay City, Saginaw, and intersects with I-69 in Flint. I-75 is very busy, bringing commuters north form Metro Detroit to the Mackinac Bridge and into the Upper Peninsula of Michigan.
- Interstate 475
- Interstate 675

U.S. Highways

- US-10 bypasses Midland and terminates at I-75 in Bay City, merging into M-25. Viewed from an east-west orientation, it provides a mainly westerly road across Northern Michigan from Bay City off I-75 toward Ludington.
- US-23 comes out of Ohio merges with I-75 south of Flint, and then breaks away at Standish. It then proceeds north, along the Lake Huron shoreline to the Mackinaw City.

Michigan Highways

- M-13 is a 72.22 mile north-south highway that cuts through the bay region of the U.S. state of Michigan. The southern terminus is at I-69 south of the town of Lennon with its northern terminus located south of Standish. It is a shorter alternative route, instead of I-75, from Bay City to US 23 in Standish.
- M-15
- M-19
- M-20
- M-21
- old M-21
- M-24
- M-25 is a highway of an arc-like shape closely following the outline of the Thumb along the Lake Huron/Saginaw Bay shoreline between Port Huron, Michigan (junction I-94, I-69, and I-94

Business Loop and Bay City, Michigan (junction I-75, US-23, and US-10. It is generally a scenic drive.
- M-29
- M-30
- M-46 is a cross peninsular road, running across the mitten and the thumb—from Port Sanilac on the Lake Huron shore; through Saginaw near Saginaw Bay; and then on to Muskegon on the Lake Michigan shore. This east-west surface route nearly bisects the Lower Peninsula of Michigan latitudinally.
- M-47
- M-53 (Van Dyke Road) is a gateway route to The Thumb of Michigan, carrying vacationers to the resorts and cottages on Saginaw Bay and Lake Huron in the vicinity of Caseville and Port Austin. It goes up the middle of the Thumb, and directly connects in Macomb County, Michigan to the M-53 expressway. It is an important route for agricultural and manufactured goods.
- M-52
- M-54 The Dort Highway, A main road leading into Flint replaced by I-475
- M-57
- M-58
- M-81
- M-83
- M-84
- M-90
- M-136
- M-138
- M-142

Rail

- Main article: Michigan Services

Area Amtrak stations are in Lapeer, Port Huron, Flint and Durand. Local railroads are the Grand Trunk Western Railroad, CSX Transport, Canadian National Rail , Pere Marquette Railway, and the Huron & Eastern Saginaw Valley Railroad.

Media

Newspapers

- Daily editions of the *Detroit Free Press* and *The Detroit News* are available throughout the area.
- Editions of the *Bay City Times*, *Midland Daily News* and *Saginaw News* are available in the greater Tri-Cities area. The *Times* and the *Saginaw News* published three times a week, while the *Midland Daily News* publishes daily. *The Great Lakes Bay Edition*, a joint publication between the *Saginaw News* and the *Bay City Times*, focuses on those two cities, as well as Midland, and publishes once a week.
- The *Flint Journal* is available in the Flint and Lapeer areas—it is published four times a week.
- The *Huron Daily Tribune* serves Huron County; it is published daily.
- The *Port Huron Times Herald* serves the lower Thumb communities; it is published daily.

Radio

The Flint/Tri-Cities area lies within four radio media markets.
- Thumb Radio Region
- Greater Tri-Cities
- Flint Area
- Detroit Area

Broadcast television

Television in Tri-Cities and Flint is mostly produced from the Flint/Tri-Cities Television Market. Far eastern areas such as Lapeer County, St. Clair County and Sanilac County lie in the Detroit Television Market. Areas like Genesee County can view programing from the Detroit and Flint/Saginaw media markets.

Availability of stations depend on reception of aerial signals, as well as availability on cable and satellite in a particular area.

Principal cities

- Tri-Cities
  - Saginaw
  - Midland
  - Bay City
- Flint
- Port Huron

Port Huron's Blue Water Bridges

See also

- List of Michigan county name etymologies
- Metro Detroit

External links

- Clarke Historical Library, Central Michigan University, Bibliography on Michigan (arranged by counties and regions) [6]
- Michigan Department of Natural Resources website. harbors, hunting, resources and more. [1]
- List of Museums, other attractions compiled by state government. [2]
- USCG's complete list of Michigan lighthouses. [3]
- Map of Michigan Lighthouse [4] in PDF format.
- Seeing the Light, Terry Pepper on lighthouses of the Western Great Lakes. [5]

History of Saginaw

History of Saginaw, Michigan

This article is about the **history of Saginaw, Michigan.**

Early history

The area of the present City of Saginaw was inhabited by woodland Native American Indians prior to settlement by those of European ancestry. The Sauk at one time lived in the area and were driven out by Ojibwe (Chippewa). The Saginaw region includes an extensive network of many rivers and streams which converge into the Saginaw River and provided a means for easy travel for the Native American population among numerous settlements and hunting areas, as well as access to Lake Huron. Saginaw was also a frequent meeting location for councils of the Ojibwe, Pottawatomi, and Ottawa.

The present City of Saginaw itself did not serve as a location for permanent settlement until the time of European contact. This may be due, in part, to the low lying and frequently flooding land adjacent to the Saginaw River, much of which was marshland prior to being drained in the 19th century. Mosquito infestation was endemic to the area.

French missionaries first reached the area in the 17th century. Henri Nouvel, a Jesuit missionary who made repeated visits to the Native Americans present in the area, is of particular significance. He recorded information concerning his travels during the 1670s in his journals. The French controlled the territory consisting of the present day State of Michigan until it was ceded to the British following the Seven Years' War in 1763. The French established permanent settlements in many locations throughout the Great Lakes, but most of the interior of the Lower Peninsula of Michigan, including the Saginaw River valley, was undeveloped. Both the French and the British primarily maintained settlements for trade and strategic defense, neither of which provided much reason to develop the Saginaw region. Following the British defeat during the American Revolutionary War, Michigan was granted to the United States. Despite this, the British remained in de facto control of the area for long after. It was not until after the conclusion of the War of 1812 that all presence of British military was removed from what is present-day Michigan. Soon after, in 1816, Louis Campau made the first attempt at permanent settlement at Saginaw by setting up a trading post. Trails leading from Detroit and the Mackinac area began to provide a slow start to Saginaw's development.

Fort Saginaw and early settlement in Saginaw

Lewis Cass in the Treaty of Saginaw negotiated the prerogative of the Americans to own and settle the area with the leaders of the Ojibwe in 1819. Soon thereafter the U.S. Army established a fort on the west bank of the Saginaw River and gave it the name Fort Saginaw. Due to the undesirable conditions of intense humidity and mosquito infestation, the Fort was abandoned by 1824 A group of investors purchased some land near the fort and had it platted under the name "Town of Sagana". Few plots were sold and after the army pulled out, the town languished for most of the following decade. The town was re-platted in December 1830, comprising river front from Cass St. on the south to Harrison St. and north to Jefferson. These plots sold slowly. By 1835, only 24 had been sold and the remainder were transferred to a new owner, who made another plat in February 1837. However, the financial crisis of the Panic of 1837 dampened interest in purchasing properties. After selling only 58 out of the 407 plots, the remainder was sold again in 1841.

Organization of county and township governments

On September 10, 1822, Territorial Governor Lewis Cass issued a proclamation that set off the boundaries of Saginaw County, although it remained attached to Oakland County for administrative purposes until there was sufficient population to organize a separate government. The county boundaries initially included what is now the southern portion of Bay County and Midland County and the northwest corner of Shiawassee County. In 1831, the northwest corner of Saginaw County was detached to become a part of Midland County. In 1835, the southeast corner was detached to become a part of Genesee County. In 1857, the northern portion was detached to become a part of Bay County, although the precise alignment of the northern boundary shifted several more times in subsequent years.

On July 12, 1830, the Territorial Legislature passed an act that erected the Township of Saginaw, effective with the first town meeting on April 4, 1831. The township comprised all of Saginaw County, which at the time was still attached to Oakland County. On January 28, 1835, the Territorial Legislature passed an act organizing county government in Saginaw County, effective on February 9, 1835.

Four years before the county government was organized, another proclamation by Governor Cass on January 11, 1831, located the county seat at what was to become the City of Saginaw. The settlement was which had been platted for that purpose by a group of area residents.

Lumber boom

The main cause for the development of Saginaw was the lumber needs of the growing American nation. A virgin growth forest principally consisting of white pine trees covered most of Michigan. The convenient access to water transportation provided by the Saginaw River and its numerous tributaries fueled a massive expansion in population and economic activity. As the trees were being felled in the region, logs were floated down the rivers to sawmills located in Saginaw, then to be loaded onto ships and later railroad cars.

Multiple settlements comprise what now is the present-day City of Saginaw. On the west side of the river the first settlement around what had been Fort Saginaw developed into Saginaw, which was incorporated as the City of Saginaw in 1857 and contained the seat of Saginaw County government. On the east side of the river a parallel settlement, East Saginaw, developed which was incorporated first as a village in 1855, and then as a city in 1859. Also south of the City of East Saginaw on the east bank of the river the Village of Salina formed. Its name relates to the salty brine that led to a growing industry of salt production in the area. Both Saginaw and East Saginaw quickly became a hub for railroad transportation in addition to ships on the Saginaw River.

Lumber production peaked by the early 1870s and had virtually disappeared by the end of the 19th century. In addition to salt production, which experienced an eventual decline as well, growing industries supporting the area's agriculture and manufacturing developed.

Consolidation of West and East sides

The former East Saginaw Post Office now is the site for the Castle Museum of Saginaw County History.

On June 28, 1889, the Michigan Legislature passed Act 455 to consolidate the City of Saginaw and the City of East Saginaw into a new city that also was named the City of Saginaw. Prior to this consolidation, the Village of Salina had already been added to the City of East Saginaw. The consolidation of the City of Saginaw became effective with the election of officers on March 12, 1890. The provisions of the city charter were established by the same act of the legislature that provided for the consolidation. The city was governed by a city council consisting of two aldermen elected from 21 wards and an executive mayor who had fairly weak powers because numerous other elected officials

and elected or appointed boards controlled much of the administrative and executive functions of government. The efficient and cohesive functioning of the City's government also was constrained by remaining rivalries between residents, business owners, and politicians from the former two cities. The distinctions and rivalries between the east and west sides of the City of Saginaw persisted throughout the ensuing century in various forms, and influences Saginaw's political and economic experiences even at the present time.

Industrial economy

At the dawn of the 20th century, production of motor vehicles became prolific throughout many communities in Michigan, but most notably Detroit. In Saginaw, the Jackson, Wilcox and Church Company produced carriages to be drawn by horses, and later produced components used in motor vehicles. The company was eventually acquired by General Motors and formed the basis for its Steering Gear division. Additionally, General Motors established foundries and other manufacturing facilities in Saginaw. The early development of automotive production within Saginaw would set the course for the future economic circumstances of the City.

Home Rule government

After a new state constitution was adopted in 1908 that mandated increased home rule powers for local units of government, the legislature enacted the Home Rule Cities Act in 1909. Under this statute, cities are permitted to frame and adopt their own city charters and are given great flexibility in structuring local government. The government under the 1889 Charter had continued to be inefficient and provided for much political infighting. In 1913, a new city charter was adopted with voter approval and which followed the commission form of city government that had gained in popular interest among various American cities in the early twentieth century. The new government consisted of five commissioners each elected separately at-large who served both as the city council and the executive heads of city government departments. One of the commissioners served as mayor, a mostly ceremonial role.

The 1913 city charter was followed for little more than two decades when the voters of the city again adopted another new city charter in 1935 following the council-manager form of government. The government under the 1913 city charter retained some of the independent boards that were given authority independent of the elected city commissioners. This caused some inefficiency and political friction. The economic consequences of the Great Depression during the 1930s provided the final catalyst for municipal government reform.

In contrast to the previous government structures, the 1935 charter, having taken effect in 1936, provided for all administration of city government to be headed directly by a single officer, the city manager, who was appointed by and accountable to a city council of nine members elected as a group by the entire city at-large. The system was designed to address two principal issues with Saginaw's history of municipal government: the inefficiency and politics associated with having executive and administrative authority spread among many different officers and boards, and political rivalries and friction between various geographic areas of the city, mainly the east and west sides.

20th century boom

As the United States entered the conflict of World War II, Saginaw's industrial complex was geared towards production supporting the war effort. Munitions and components for military vehicles made Saginaw a significant contributor to the nation's eventual victory. Specifically, Saginaw was home to one production facility that produced over half a million M1 Carbine rifles for the US Military during World War II.

Saginaw became the destination for a great number of workers migrating from areas of the United States that were greatly devastated by the Great Depression, especially from the south. This migration continued throughout the war years and in the economic boom, which followed. Saginaw, like most of America, benefited from the dramatic economic prosperity following the war. General Motors expanded its presence in Saginaw, and other manufacturers increased production as well. This caused the population of the City to swell to its height of approximately 100,000 during the 1960s.

The needs of a growing city were met by significant investment in Saginaw's infrastructure. Notably, Saginaw constructed a 65-mile long water supply pipeline drawing water from Lake Huron in 1947 to meet the anticipated needs of the community. In addition, the cities of Midland and Bay City along with Saginaw jointly developed and began to operate an airport facility in nearby Tittabawassee Township that is now MBS International Airport.

Late 20th century decline

In the years following World War II, the legislature of the State of Michigan enacted laws making it increasingly difficult for incorporated cities to expand by annexing adjacent territory contained within townships. Townships, which had historically served a rural population, were given the ability to provide nearly all of the same services that an incorporated city can. Residential growth in neighboring townships led the City of Saginaw to provide water under long-term contracts to such other units of government. This increased the ability of adjacent townships to further develop. The unintended consequence of this was that the city of Saginaw stopped growing in population and new housing development slowed significantly.

As a result of migrations of workers from other parts of the United States, particularly the south, Saginaw's African-American population expanded significantly in proportion to those of European ancestry. Attitudes of racism promoted the segregation of African-American residents into concentrated neighborhoods almost exclusively within the city's east side. Mortgage lenders and real estate sales agents enforced racial segregation by making it difficult for residents of certain areas to obtain financing or for African-Americans to purchase properties in white neighborhoods. Gradually most of the east side's white population migrated either to the west side or to adjacent townships thus making the Saginaw River the virtual dividing line for segregated racial groups in Saginaw. From the 1950s onward and persisting to the present, African-Americans overwhelmingly comprise the east side's population while white residents form a majority of the west side. After the eventual breakdown of institutionally enforced segregation and increased opportunities for African-Americans, however, the west side has become significantly more diverse in its ethnic and racial composition and no longer has almost exclusively white residents.

The geographic racial segregation within Saginaw set the stage for much of the city's political concerns during the last 40 years. Increasingly, race and ethnicity became significant aspects of local political campaigns and issues. The racial composition of the majority of the city council has shifted between African-Americans and whites during this time. This has caused for some degree of tension to exist among members of the council at various times. The city council appoints a replacement member in the event of a vacancy. In each instance where a vacancy has occurred under the present city charter, a white replacement has been appointed when a white council member has vacated the seat, and an African-American replacement has been appointed when the prior incumbent was of the same race.[citation needed]

Also, since the city council selects one of its own members to serve as mayor, the racial group with a majority of the city council membership has elected a mayor from the same racial group. From 1989 until 2005, a majority of the city council membership was African-American and each of the mayors serving during this time were also African-Americans Gary L. Loster served the longest tenure of any mayor in Saginaw's history during this time, an unprecedented four terms from 1993 until 2001.

The economic conditions of the City of Saginaw make up another significant area of concern. The decline of manufacturing has resulted in high rates of unemployment. There has been a decline in the values of properties in the city, which has shrunk the amount the city is able to collect through property taxes. Saginaw has experienced a significant rate of crime activity while at the same time being forced to decrease the size of its police department. Overall, the number of employees and size and scope of city government is now nearly half of its level during the 1970s.

See also
- Saginaw Trail

Things to See In and Around Saginaw

Temple Theatre (Saginaw, Michigan)

The **Temple Theatre** is a historic theater built by the Elf Khurafeh Shriners and opened in 1927 in Saginaw, Michigan. The theater was restored in late 2002 and reopened under new owners to host events in the Saginaw area.

Events

The Temple Theatre has hosted a variety of entertainers. In 2006, Jim Brickman, Three Men and a Tenor, and George Carlin graced the stage of the historic Temple Theatre.

The Temple Theatre also shows a number of films on the big screen. The Muppet Christmas Carol, White Christmas, Miracle on 34th Street, and Peter Jackson's King Kong were shown in late 2006.

External links

- Temple Theatre Homepage [1]

Castle Museum (Saginaw, Michigan)

Castle Station	
U.S. National Register of Historic Places	
The Castle Museum of Saginaw County History	
Location:	S. Jefferson at Federal St., Saginaw, Michigan
Coordinates:	43°25′43″N 83°56′9″W
Built/Founded:	1897
Architect:	Aiken, William M.; Macomber, Carl
Architectural style(s):	Renaissance, Other
Governing body:	Federal (General Services Administration)
Added to NRHP:	January 13, 1972
NRHP Reference#:	72000652

The **Castle Museum**, previously known as **Castle Station** or **Saginaw Post Office**, in Saginaw, Michigan, USA is a historic structure on the National Register of Historic Places. It is currently the home of the Historical Society of Saginaw County and officially known as the **Castle Museum of Saginaw County History**.

History

The Castle Museum was designed by William Martin Aiken, the Supervising Architect of the US Treasury, and built in 1898 as a United States Post Office. In the 1930s, the post office was becoming too small and a movement was started to get the post office out and into another building. An uproar arose because no one wanted their beloved castle to be torn down. The building was remodeled by local architect Carl Macomber, who enlarged the building, tore down one of the three turrets, and added a large sorting room on the back of the building (by Hoyt Library). In the 1970s, a new post office was built and the building was almost demolished once again, but local citizens and the Saginaw County Board of Commissioners took steps to list the building on the National Register of Historic Places to ensure the preservation of the building and the local heritage it represents.

The Castle Museum and Annex is located at 500 Federal Avenue, Saginaw, MI 48607. Phone: (989) 752-2861 Fax: (989) 752-1533.

External links

- Historical Society of Saginaw County and the Castle Museum official site. [10]

Fashion Square Mall

Location	Saginaw Charter Township, Michigan, U.S.
Coordinates	43°28′36″N 83°58′22″W
Address	4787 Fashion Square Mall
Opening date	1972
Management	CBL & Associates Properties
No. of stores and services	100+
No. of anchor tenants	3
Total retail floor area	798016 square feet (74138 m^2)
Parking	5235
No. of floors	1
Website	Official website [1]

Fashion Square Mall is an enclosed shopping mall located in the northern edge of Saginaw Charter Township, Michigan. It lies within the boundaries of M-84 (Bay Road) to the west, Tittabawassee Road to the north, Fashion Square Blvd. to the east, and Schust Road to the south. The mall serves city of Saginaw and surrounding suburban areas. It features more than 100 tenants, including a food court, and its anchor stores are JCPenney, Macy's and Sears. CBL & Associates Properties manages Fashion Square Mall.

History

Fashion Square Mall opened in 1972 with J.C. Penney and Sears as its major anchor stores. Hudson's, a chain based in Detroit, Michigan, was added in 1976 to the eastern end, as a third major anchor. The mall also included branches of two local department stores: William C. Weichmann Company and Heavenrich's, the former of which was liquidated in 1992.

A $10 million mall-wide renovation was completed in 2001, with the addition of new seating areas, family restrooms, and automatic doors. The same year, reflecting nameplate consolidation by Hudson's parent Target Corp., the mall's eastern anchor was re-branded as Marshall Field's, and by 2006, Marshall Field's would be among several nameplates to be converted to the Macy's name. Dunham's Sports also moved out in the 2000s, with Steve & Barry's taking its place in 2005. Steve & Barry's closed in December 2008 after the chain declared bankruptcy. McDonald's closed its food court location in January 2009, as did a Garfield's restaurant in May, only six months after opening in a space vacated by Ruby Tuesday.

In January 2010, the J.C. Penney store underwent a remodel, including the addition of a Sephora cosmetics store.

Lawsuit

In 1981, the mall was part of a lawsuit involving the lease of an Elias Bros. Big Boy restaurant which operated within.

External links

- Official website [1]

Attractions

Saginaw Trail

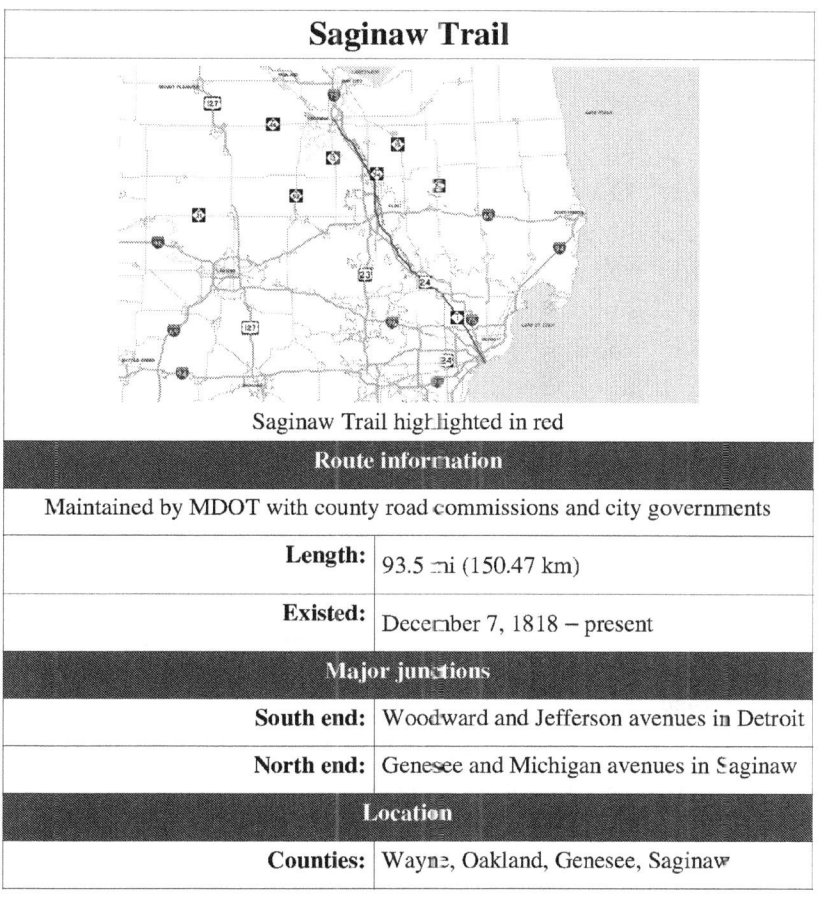

Saginaw Trail	
Saginaw Trail highlighted in red	
Route information	
Maintained by MDOT with county road commissions and city governments	
Length:	93.5 mi (150.47 km)
Existed:	December 7, 1818 – present
Major junctions	
South end:	Woodward and Jefferson avenues in Detroit
North end:	Genesee and Michigan avenues in Saginaw
Location	
Counties:	Wayne, Oakland, Genesee, Saginaw

Saginaw Trail is the collective name for a set of connected roads in Southeastern Michigan that runs from Detroit to Saginaw through Pontiac and Flint. It was originally a foot trail created by the Sauk Tribe. On December 7, 1818 the Michigan Territorial government authorized the building of a road from Detroit to Saginaw along the trail. The road has gone through a number of designation changes in the last two centuries, both in name and number. Since the Michigan portion of Interstate 75 (I-75) was completed in 1973, it has been a secondary route.

Today, drivers can follow the path of the Saginaw Trail starting with Woodward Avenue in Detroit north to Genesee Avenue in Saginaw. It is currently state-maintained as different sections of state trunkline highways bearing the designations M-1, US Highway 24 (US 24) and M-54. Other sections are maintained as county roads or city streets. Several landmarks can be found on these roads, and numerous historical events have taken place on them. The road has also been featured in some films and TV shows.

History

The original trail

Sauk Tribal foot path

The Sauk tribe may have had their original territory along the St. Lawrence River. However, migration patterns of other tribes drove them to Michigan around Saginaw Bay. Due to the yellow clay soils found around Saginaw Bay, their self-designation became *OƟaakiiwaki* which is often interpreted to mean "yellow-earth". The Ojibwe and Ottawa name for the tribe is *Ozaagii*, meaning "Those at the Outlet", whence they were known by the French as "Sac" or by the English as "Sauk". With the Anishinaabe expansion and Hurons attempts at gaining regional stability, the Sauks were driven away by the Hurons armed with French weapons. The Sauk then occupied territory in parts of what are now northern Illinois and Wisconsin.

The Sauk tribe created an unnamed foot trail from Detroit to Saginaw. When European settlers arrived, they too began using the trail, which they dubbed the Saginaw Trail. These settlers determined the government should modernize it for the use of their horses and carriages. The name Saginaw is believed to mean "where the Sauk were" in the Ojibwe language, which is used by the Chippewa tribe.

Government builds a road

The Michigan Territorial Legislature approved the building of the Saginaw Turnpike (also called the Detroit–Saginaw Turnpike) on December 7, 1818. Michigan Territory Governor Lewis Cass established by proclamation on December 15, 1819 the building of the section from Saginaw to Pontiac. The Legislature approved the request to build the southern half, from Pontiac to Detroit, on June 22, 1822. However, the Michigan government could not find the needed money in its budget to do so. Therefore, in 1826, the Michigan Territory asked for federal money to do so. After months of consideration, the federal government approved the request on March 2, 1827. The Detroit to Flint section was finished in 1833, and the Flint to Saginaw section was finished in 1841.

Private ownership

In 1848 and 1850, the Michigan government determined it was too expensive to maintain the road, and therefore turned it over to a private plank company who kept it up, in return for tolls to travel on it. Tolls on the road were regulated by the state legislature. A charge of two cents a mile was made for a wagon or carriage drawn by two horses, and one cent a mile for every sled or sleigh so drawn. If more than two horses were used, an additional charge of three-quarters of a cent per mile for each additional animal was levied. A toll of one cent per mile was made for a vehicle drawn by one horse, as well as for a horse and rider. Tolls of one-half cent a mile were levied for every score of sheep or swine; for every score of "neat cattle," two cents a mile. Sixty years later in 1910, the leases expired and the road was turned back over to state control, at which time all fees were lifted.

State controls the road again

In 1909, Woodward Avenue between Six Mile Road and Seven Mile Road became the first mile (1.6 km) of paved highway in the United States. In 1916, the 27-mile (43 km) portion of Woodward from Detroit to Pontiac was paved. The nation's first tri-colored traffic light was installed on Woodward in 1919. Portions of the trail were part of the Dixie Highway from 1915 to 1927. From 1919 to 1926, the trail was designated M-10.

Starting in 1926, when the U.S. Highway System was created, US 10 ran along the trail. The section between Downtown Flint and Saginaw also carried US 23. In 1928, the segment between Dort Highway's northern terminus and Dort Highway's former southern terminus was changed to M-10, which was the second incarnation of M-10. In 1941 or 1942, that designation of M-10 was changed to Business US 10 (BUS US 10). In 1957, US 23 was moved from the trail to its current route.

Several changes were made to the Saginaw Trail in 1962. US 10 and BUS US 10 were removed from I-75 exit 106 to Dort Highway's northern terminus. M-54 opened, running along Saginaw Street between I-75 exit 106, through Grand Blanc to Dort Highway's former southern terminus. Saginaw Street between Dort Highway's former southern terminus and northern terminus was renamed BUS M-54. The designation of US 10 between the former southern terminus of M-54 and Clarkston was moved to the new I-75 freeway.

In 1970, US 10 was moved between Pontiac and Detroit, and Woodward Avenue was redesignated as M-1. US 10 was routed along the Lodge Freeway and Telegraph Road. The BUS M-54 signs were removed in 1984 along Saginaw Street. US 10 was truncated in 1986, removing the designation from the highway system south of Bay City. The section of M-54 from Dort Highway's former southern terminus was rerouted along a new extension and M-54 no longer ran along Saginaw Street through Grand Blanc like it did previously, making its current southern terminus at I-75 exit 109 in 1987.

Saginaw Trail Cleaners on Dixie Highway in Waterford pays homage to the road's original name

Evidence of the Saginaw Trail today

Evidence of the original Saginaw Trail path through Royal Oak is still visible as a depression in the ground running northwesterly across the property adjacent of the John Almon Starr House. The Starr house, located at 3123 Crooks Road, is approximately 1 mile (about 1 1/2 km) east of Woodward Avenue. The road was constructed along (but not always over) the original trail, by order of the Michigan government. A Michigan Historical Marker for the Saginaw Trail is co-located with that of the John Almon Starr House.

In Waterford, there is a dry cleaners on Dixie Highway called "Saginaw Trail Cleaners".

There is a 1953 film starring Gene Autry named *Saginaw Trail*, set in Michigan during 19th century fur trading days.

Route description

Wayne County

The old Saginaw Trail is known as Woodward Avenue (M-1) in Wayne County. Woodward Avenue starts in Downtown Detroit at Jefferson Avenue near the Renaissance Center, the world headquarters of the General Motors Corporation. From this starting point, the street runs northwesterly through Downtown Detroit, passing through Campus Martius Park and Grand Circus Park. The north side of the latter park is on Adams Avenue, which marks the start of the M-1 designation and state maintenance. The historic Fox Theatre, which was

Comerica Park in Downtown Detroit is near the trail

built in 1928, is on Woodward Avenue, and next door to it is The Fillmore Detroit, a concert venue. Across the street is Comerica Park, home of the Detroit Tigers. Next to it is Ford Field, home of the Detroit Lions. Both sports venues are west of Woodward Avenue, between Adams and the I-75 freeway. Further north is the Detroit Institute of Arts.

Woodward Avenue continues northwesterly crossing through the campus of Wayne State University and the city of Highland Park before re-entering Detroit at McNichols Road,

The historic Fox Theatre is on Woodward

which occupies the 6 Mile location in the Mile Road System in Detroit. At 8 Mile Road, Woodward Avenue crosses out of Detroit for the final time near the State Fairgrounds into Ferndale and Oakland County.

Woodward Avenue in Detroit has been mentioned in popular culture several times, such as in the season-6 episode of the Detroit-based 1990s sitcom *Home Improvement* titled 'My Son, the Driver". The character Brad mentions he was "rear-ended over on Woodward". Woodward is also known internationally for its annual "Woodward Dream Cruise" in which classic car enthusiasts showcase their vehicles.

Oakland County

Woodward Avenue continues north toward Pontiac. It passes through the suburbs of Ferndale, Royal Oak, Birmingham and Bloomfield Hills. Royal Oak is the location of the John Almon Starr House which is adjacent to the original trail. In Bloomfield Hills, the M-1 designation ends at Square Lake Road. Woodward Avenue continues north into downtown Pontiac as part of Business Loop I-75 (BL I-75) and BUS US 24. Through downtown, the highway splits along two streets of a one-way pair, using Woodward Avenue northbound and Wide Track Drive southbound. BL I-75 turns off along Perry Street, and BUS US 24 continues north along Oakland Avenue northbound and Cass Avenue southbound. The two streets merge together along Oakland Avenue north of Montcalm Street. North of Kennett Road, the street name changes to Dixie Highway.

Dixie Highway was named as a part of the original auto trail of the same name. When the road meets Telegraph Road, it loses the BUS US 24 designation in favor of US 24. Dixie Highway, and the Saginaw Trail, pass a number of lakes north of Pontiac before meeting I-75 in Independence Township at exit 93. This is the eastern end of US 24, which runs 2478 miles (3988 km), all the way from Colorado Springs, Colorado. Dixie Highway continues northwesterly and parallels I-75, using roadway that was once US 10. The grounds for the annual Michigan Renaissance Festival, which is unofficially dubbed "Hollygrove" for the festival, are located on Dixie Highway in both Holly Township and Groveland Township. The festival grounds was the primary shooting location of the 2009 romantic comedy film *All's Faire in Love*. Mount Holly Ski Area is also located on Dixie Highway in Holly

Township. Groveland Oaks County Park, which features a spiraling water-slide, is also on the roadway in Groveland Township. The Michigan State Police's Satellite Office 21 is located next to Dixie Highway in Groveland Township.

Genesee County

In Genesee County, it is known as Saginaw Road or Saginaw Street. South of the Flint River, it is designated South Saginaw Street or South Saginaw Road, and north of the river, it is designated North Saginaw Street or North Saginaw Road. In Grand Blanc Township, Warwick Hills Golf and Country Club, former home of the PGA's Buick Open (which has now been discontinued) is on Saginaw Road. Also on Saginaw Road in Grand Blanc Township is a branch office of the 67th District Court and Grand Blanc Township's Administrative Offices. In southern Flint, on Saginaw Street between Atherton and Hemphill Roads, is the Fisher Body Plant #1, which is now the Great Lakes Technology Center. This plant was the site of the Flint Sit-Down Strike, a pivotal event in the development of the United Auto Workers.

Citizens Republic Bancorp's headquarters on Saginaw Street in Downtown Flint

In Downtown Flint several government buildings are on Saginaw Street, including the historic 1917 Genesee County Circuit Courthouse, Flint City Hall, the Genesee County Administration Building, the Genesee County Jail, the Genesee County Sheriff's Department headquarters, the headquarters of the 67th and 68th District Courts, and the Genesee County Health Department. The headquarters of Citizens Republic Bancorp which was founded as Citizens Commercial & Savings Bank in Flint in 1871 are on Saginaw Street in Downtown Flint, as is the historic First National Bank of Flint which was founded in 1864. The current building was constructed in 1924.

Another popular culture reference to the Saginaw Trail came In the 2008 movie *Semi-Pro*, which was filmed partially in Flint. The main character Jackie Moon, played by Will Ferrell, was shown driving on Saginaw Street at the Flint River bridge in Downtown Flint.

Continuing north through the county, in Mount Morris, a branch office of the 67th District Court is on Saginaw Street, as well as the Mount Morris City Administration Offices. Auto City Speedway is on Saginaw Road between Mount Morris and Clio. Between Dort Highway's northern terminus and Clio Road in Genesee County, Saginaw Road is part of M-54.

Saginaw County

In Saginaw County, it is also known as Dixie Highway, except in the City of Saginaw, where it is known as Genesee Avenue. In this segment, the road mostly runs through farmlands and rural residential areas. The Michigan State Police has 2 offices on the trail in Saginaw County: Post 37 is on Dixie Highway in Bridgeport Township, and the District 3 headquarters are on Genesee Avenue in Saginaw. Dixie Motor Speedway is on Dixie Highway in Birch Run Township. and a few miles north in in Bridgeport Township is the Bridgeport Township Administration Office. Also in Bridgeport is the Junction Valley Railroad, the world's largest quarter scale railroad system. The trail ends at Michigan Avenue in Downtown Saginaw.

Major intersectons

County	Location	Mile	Destinations	Notes
Wayne	Detroit	0.0	M-10 (Jefferson Avenue)	Southern terminus of the Saginaw Trail
		0.7	Adams Avenue	Southern terminus of M-1; state maintenance begins
		2.7	I-94 west (Ford Freeway) - Chicago	No access to eastbound I-94
		5.8	M-8 (Davison Freeway)	
		9.2	M-102 (8 Mile Road)	8 Mile is the border between Wayne and Oakland counties
Oakland	Royal Oak	11.3	I-696 (Walter P. Reuther Freeway) – Lansing, Port Huron	
	Pontiac	22.2	BL I-75 / BUS US 24 (Square Lake Road)	Northern terminus of M-1; Woodward Avenue continues into Downtown Pontiac as BL I-75/BUS US 24
		25.0	M-59 (Huron Street)	
		25.5	BL I-75 (Perry Street)	Northern end of BL I-75 concurrency
	Waterford Township	27.9	US 24 (Dixie Highway)	BUS US 24 ends; Saginaw Trail follows US 24/Dixie Highway
	Independence Township	34.0	M-15 north (Main Street) – Clarkston	Southern terminus of M-15
	Springfield Township	36.2	I-75 – Flint, Detroit	US 24 ends at exit 98; state maintenance ends and Dixie Highway continues as a county road

County	Location	Mile	Destinations	Notes
Genesee	Grand Blanc Township	48.0	I-75 – Flint, Detroit	Exit 106 on the Oakland–Genesee County line; Saginaw Trail is known as Saginaw Road or Saginaw Street in Genesee County
		48.7	M-54 (Dort Highway) – Flint	
	Flint	59.2	I-69 – Lansing, Port Huron	Exit 138
		59.6	M-21 (Court Street)	
	Mount Morris Township	65.8	I-475 – Saginaw, Detroit	Exit 13
	Vienna Township	69.2	M-54 south (Dort Highway) – Flint	M-54 joins Saginaw Road; state maintenance begins again
		71.3	M-57 (Vienna Road) – Clio, Montrose	
		73.4	M-54 north (Clio Road) – Birch Run	M-54 turns north on Clio Road, leaving Saginaw Road; state maintenance ends again
Saginaw	Birch Run Township	77.0	M-54 / M-83 – Birch Run, Frankenmuth	Just east of I-75 exit 136
	Bridgeport	85.5	I-75 / US 23 – Saginaw, Flint	Exit 144
	Saginaw	91.0	M-46 east (Holland Avenue) – Sandusky	Saginaw Trail changes street names to Genesee Avenue in the City of Saginaw
		91.1	M-46 west (Remington Street) – Alma	M-46 is routed on a one-way pair of streets here in Saginaw
		92.6	M-13 (Washington Avenue) – Bay City	
		93.5	Michigan Avenue	Northern terminus of the Saginaw Trail

See also

- Sauk Trail
- Mackinac Trail

References

- Ashlee, Laura Rose (2005). *Traveling Through Time: A Guide to Michigan's Historical Markers*. Ann Arbor, MI: University of Michigan Press. p. 346.
- Barnett, Ph.D., LeRoy (2004). *A Drive Down Memory Lane: The Named State and Federal Highways of Michigan*. Allegan Forest, MI: Priscilla Press. pp. 192–3. ISBN 1-886167-24-9.

- Mason, Philip P. (Wayne State University) (1986). *The Plank Road Craze: A Chapter in the History of Michigan's Highways* [1]. Michigan Department of History, Arts & Libraries. Retrieved August 30, 2009.

External links

- M-1 at Michigan Highways [2]
- M-10 at Michigan Highways [3]
- US 24 at Michigan Highways [4]
- M-54 at Michigan Highways [5]

Saginaw River

The **Saginaw River** is a 22-mile-long (35 km) river in the U.S. state of Michigan. It is formed by the confluence of the Tittabawassee and Shiawassee rivers southeast of Saginaw. It flows northward into the Saginaw Bay of Lake Huron just northeast of Bay City.

The river is an important shipping route for Mid-Michigan, passing through the cities of Saginaw and Bay City. It is one of Michigan's few inland navigable rivers.

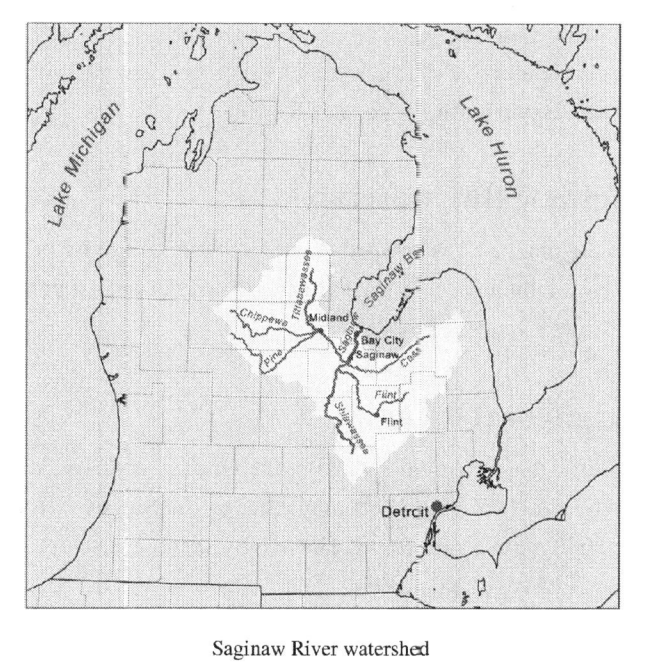

Saginaw River watershed

Recreational Activities

The Saginaw River is popular with recreational boaters and fishermen. It is home to the annual Shiver on the River [1] walleye ice fishing contest. Each winter, trophy-sized fish are taken through the ice and again early in the spring. The Saginaw Bay Yacht Club is located near the mouth of the Saginaw river.

Tens of thousands flock to its banks for annual festivals such as the River Roar speed boat races and two of the largest fireworks displays in the Midwest.

A three-mile, hard-surfaced RiverWalk that is great for hiking, biking or just easy strolls is featured along the riverbanks in downtown Saginaw and Bay City.

Pollution

The Saginaw River and its watershed have been polluted with various wastes discharged into the Saginaw river and its tributaries from several sources. The Dow Chemical Company, General Motors, City of Bay City, and the City of Saginaw have contributed to the release of dioxins into the Saginaw River. Agricultural and various other activities result in the release of even more chemicals and other toxic wastes into the river.

Saginaw Bay

Saginaw Bay is a bay within Lake Huron located on the eastern side of the U.S. state of Michigan. It forms the space between Michigan's Thumb region and the rest of the Lower Peninsula of Michigan. Saginaw Bay is 1143 square miles (2960 km^2) in area. It is located in parts of five Michigan counties: Arenac, Bay, Huron, Iosco, and Tuscola.

Saginaw Bay watershed

The Saginaw Bay watershed is the largest drainage basin in Michigan, draining approximately 15% of the total land area. The watershed contains the largest contiguous freshwater coastal wetland system in the United States.

Origin of the name

O-Sag-e-non or *Sag-in-a-we* from the Ojibwa language, which means "to flow out", is a possible origin for the name "Saginaw". It may refer to the Saginaw River, which flows out into Saginaw Bay, and eventually into Lake Huron. The name "Saginaw" is not related to Saguenay, a region in Quebec whose name is of Algonquin origin.

History

The modern history of Saginaw Bay dates back to early 17th century. French explorers were the first Europeans to visit the Great Lakes region.

The first European to visit the Saginaw Bay area was Father Jacques Marquette, a French missionary priest, who came here in 1668 after establishing a mission in St. Ignace. In 1686, Father Jean Enjalran came to the valley to establish an Indian mission, but his efforts failed.

The region was ceded to Great Britain under the terms of the Treaty of Paris of 1763. Twenty years later, it was ceded to the newly-independent United States of America. It became part of the Michigan Territory in 1805.

Settlements

About 1813, Louis Campau erected an Indian trading post along the Saginaw River which led to the settlement of Saginaw in 1816, and to which the history of other settlements of Saginaw Bay area are rooted.

Bay City, Michigan is a major port at the lower end of the bay. The two Charity Islands in the middle of the bay, Charity Island and Little Charity Island, are excellent fishing grounds.

Weather

Saginaw Bay Light No. 1, a navigational light near the mouth of the Saginaw River, houses NOAA weather equipment providing weather conditions for the Bay. Gravelly Shoal Light, located near Charity Island, also houses a weather station.

Culture

- A World War II escort carrier was named *Saginaw Bay*.
- The Saginaw Bay Yacht Club remains one of the most prestigious in the region.

External links

- Beacons in the Night, Michigan Lighthouse Chronology, Clarke Historical Library, Central Michigan University. [13]

Geographical coordinates: 43°55′N 83°35′W

Lake Huron

Lake Huron	

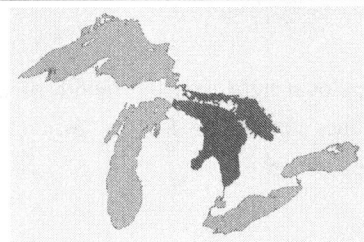	
Map of Lake Huron and the other Great Lakes	
Location	North America
Group	Great Lakes
Coordinates	44°48′N 82°24′W
Lake type	Glacial
Primary inflows	Straits of Mackinac, St. Marys River
Primary outflows	St. Clair River
Catchment area	193473 km^2 (74700 sq mi)
Basin countries	Canada, United States
Max. length	332 km (206 mi)
Max. width	245 km (152 mi)
Surface area	59596 km^2 (23010 sq mi)
Average depth	59 m (194 ft)
Max. depth	228.6 m (750 ft)
Water volume	3539 km^3 (849 cu mi)
Residence time	22 years

Lake Huron

Shore length[1]	6156 km (3825 mi)
Surface elevation	176 m (577 ft)
Islands	Manitoulin
Sections/sub-basins	Georgian Bay, North Channel
Settlements	Bay City, Alpena, Cheboygan, St. Ignace, Port Huron in Michigan; Goderich, Sarnia in Ontario
References	

[1] Shore length is not a well-defined measure.

Lake Huron (French: *Lac Huron*) is one of the five Great Lakes of North America. Geologically, it comprises the larger portion of Lake Michigan-Huron. It is bounded on the east by the Canadian province of Ontario and on the west by the state of Michigan in the United States. The name of the lake is derived from early French explorers who named it based on the Huron people inhabiting the region.

Geography

Lake Huron is the second largest of the Great Lakes, with a surface area of 59,596 km^2 (23,010 sq mi) making it the third largest fresh water lake on earth (fourth largest lake if the saline Caspian Sea is included). It contains a volume of 3,540 km^3 (850 cubic miles), and a shoreline length of 3,827 mi (6,157 km).

The surface of Lake Huron is 577 ft (176 m) above sea level. The lake's average depth is 195 ft (59 m), while the maximum depth is 750 ft (229 m). It has a length of 206 mi (332 km) and a greatest breadth of 183 mi (293 km).

Important cities on Lake Huron include: Goderich, Sarnia, Bay City, Alpena, Rogers City, Cheboygan, St. Ignace, and Port Huron.[citation needed]

A notable feature of the lake is Manitoulin Island, which separates the North Channel and Georgian Bay from Lake Huron's main body of water. It is the world's largest freshwater island.

Water Levels

Historic High Water The lake fluctuates from month to month with the highest lake levels in October and November. The normal highwater mark is 2.00 feet (0.61 m) above datum (*577.5 ft or 176.0 meters*). In the summer of 1986, Lakes Michigan and Huron reached their highest level at 5.92 feet (1.80 m) above datum. The high water records began in February 1986 and lasted through the year, ending with January 1987. Water levels ranged from 3.67 feet (1.12 m) to 5.92 feet (1.80 m) above Chart Datum.

Historic Low Water Lake levels tend to be the lowest in winter. The normal lowwater mark is 1.00 foot (0.30 m) below datum (*577.5 ft or 176.0 meters*). In the winter of 1964, Lakes Michigan and Huron reached their lowest level at 1.38 feet (0.42 m) below datum. As with the highwater records, monthly low water records were set each month from February 1964 through January 1965. During this twelve month period water levels ranged from 1.38 feet (0.42 m) to 0.71 feet (0.22 m) below Chart Datum.

Great Lakes Circle Tour

The Great Lakes Circle Tour is a designated scenic road system connecting all of the Great Lakes and the St. Lawrence River.

Geology

Lake Huron is separated from Lake Michigan, which lies at the same level, by the narrow Straits of Mackinac, making them geologically and hydrologically the same body of water (sometimes called Lake Michigan-Huron). Lake Superior is slightly higher than both. It drains into the St. Marys River at Sault Ste. Marie which then flows southward into Lake Huron. The water then flows south to the St. Clair River, at Port Huron, Michigan and Sarnia, Ontario.

The Great Lakes Waterway continues thence to Lake St. Clair; the Detroit River and Detroit, Michigan; into Lake Erie and thence – via Lake Ontario and the St. Lawrence River – to the Atlantic Ocean.

Like the other Great Lakes, it was formed by melting ice as the continental glaciers retreated toward the end of the last ice age. Before this, Lake Huron was a low-lying depression through which flowed the now-buried Laurentian and Huronian Rivers; the lake bed was criss-crossed by a large network of tributaries to these ancient waterways, with many of the old channels still evident on bathymetric maps.

History

The French, the first European visitors to the region, often referred to Lake Huron as La Mer Douce, "the fresh-water sea". In 1656, a map by French cartographer Nicolas Sanson, refers to the lake as Karegnondi, a Wendat word which has been variously translated as "Freshwater Sea", "Lake of the Hurons", or simply "lake".

The lake was generally labeled "Lac des Hurons" (Lake of the Huron) on most early European maps.

Storm of 1913

Main articles: Great Lakes Storm of 1913 and Great Storms of the North American Great Lakes

On November 9, 1913, a great storm in Lake Huron sank ten ships and more than twenty were driven ashore. The storm, which raged for 16 hours, killed 235 seamen.

The Matoa had passed between Port Huron, Michigan and Sarnia, Ontario just after midnight. On the 9th, just after six in the morning, the Senator pushed upstream. Less than an hour later, the Manola passed through. Captain Frederick W. Light of the Manola reported that both the

Ipperwash Beach, Lake Huron

Canadian and the American weather stations had storm flag signals flying from their weather towers. Following behind at 7:00 a.m. that Sunday, the Regina steamed out of Sarnia into the northwest gale. The warnings now had been up for four hours. The Manola passed the Regina off Port Sanilac, 22 miles up the lake. Captain Light determined that if it continued to deteriorate, he would seek shelter at Harbor Beach, Michigan, another 30 miles up the lake. There, he could seek shelter behind the breakwater. Before reaching Harbor Beach, the winds turned to the northeast and the lake began to rise. It would be noon before he reached Harbor Beach and ran for shelter. The waves were so violent that the Manola touched bottom entering the harbor. With help from a tug, the Manola tied up to the break wall with eight lines. It was about 3:00 p.m. when the Manola was secured and the crew prepared to drop anchor. As they worked, the cables began to snap from wind pressure against the hull. To keep from being pushed aground, they kept their bow into the wind with the engines running half to full in turns, yet the ship still drifted 800 feet before its movement was arrested. Waves breaking over the ship damaged several windows and the crew reported seeing portions of the concrete break wall peeling off as the waves struck it.

Meanwhile, fifty miles further up the lake, the Matoa, and Captain Hugh McLeod had to ride out the storm without a safe harbor The Matoa would be found stranded on the Port Austin reef when the winds subsided. It was noon on Monday before the winds let up and not until 11:00 p.m. that night before Capt. Light determined it to be safe to continue his journey.

Shipwrecks

See also: Shipwrecks in the Great Lakes

More than a thousand wrecks have been recorded in Lake Huron. These purportedly include the first European vessel to sail the Great Lakes, Le Griffon built in 1679 on the eastern shore of Lake Erie, near Buffalo, New York, Sieur de la Salle navigated across Lake Erie, up the Detroit River, Lake St. Clair and the St. Clair River out into Lake Huron. Passing the Straits of Mackinac, La Salle and the *Griffon* made landfall on Washington Island, off the tip of the Door Peninsula on the Wisconsin side of Lake Michigan. Here, La Salle filled the *Griffon* with pelts and in late November 1679 sent the *Griffon* back to the site of modern day Buffalo, never to be seen again.

Two wrecks have been identified as the *Griffon*, although neither has gained final verification as the actual wreck. Blown by a fierce storm after leaving, the *Griffon* ran aground before the storm. The people of Manitoulin Island say that the wreck in Mississagi Straits at the western tip of the island is that of the *Griffon*. Meanwhile, others near Tobermory say that the wreck on Russell Island, 150 miles further east in Georgian Bay is that of the Griffin.

Saginaw Bay

185 of 1000+ wrecks are within the waters of Saginaw Bay.

Matoa, A propeller freighter, 2,311 gross tons, built 1890, Cleveland, wrecked, **1913**, Port Austin Reef

Georgian Bay, North Channel

Georgian Bay, which is the largest bay on Lake Huron, contains the most wrecks in Lake Huron, of the 1000 sunk vessels, 212 lie here.

Manola, a propeller freighter of 2,325 gross tons. Built in 1890, by the Globe Shipping Company of Cleveland, Ohio. Operated by the Minnesota Steamship Company (Cleveland) from 1890–1901, by the Pittsburgh Steamship Company from 1901-1918. On January 25, 1918, the Manola was sold to the U.S. Shipping Board. It was sold again in 1920 to the Canada Steamship Lines, Ltd and renamed the **Mapledawn**. It became stranded on November 20, 1924 on Christian Island in Georgian Bay. It was headed for Port McNichol, Ontario. It was declared a total loss after two weeks. Salvagers were able to recover c.75,000 bushels of barley for delivery to Midland, Ontario.

View of rocky shore of Lake Huron from east of Port Dolomite, Michigan in the upper peninsula.

Ecology

Lake Huron has a lake retention time of 22 years.

Like all of the Great Lakes, the ecology of Lake Huron has undergone drastic changes in the last century. The lake originally supported a native deepwater fish community dominated by lake trout, which fed on a number of deepwater ciscos as well as sculpins and other native fishes. Several invasive species, including sea lamprey, alewife and rainbow smelt, became abundant in the lake by the 1930s. The major native top predator, lake trout, were virtually extirpated from the lake by 1950 due to a combination of overfishing and the effects of sea lamprey. Several species of deepwater ciscos were also extirpated from the lake by the 1960s; the only remaining native deepwater cisco is the bloater. Nonnative Pacific salmon have been stocked in the lake since the 1960s, and lake trout have also been stocked in an attempt to rehabilitate the species, although little natural reproduction of stocked trout has been observed.

Lake Huron has suffered recently due the introduction of a variety of new invasive species, including zebra and quagga mussels, the spiny water flea, and round gobies. The deepwater demersal fish community of the lake was in a state of collapse by 2006, and a number of drastic changes have been observed in the zooplankton community of the lake. Chinook salmon catches have also been greatly reduced in recent years, and lake whitefish have become less abundant and are in poor condition. These recent changes may be attributable to the new exotic species.

See also

- Drummond Island
- Georgian Bay
- Hurricane Huron
- Les Cheneaux Islands
- Mackinac Island
- Michigan lighthouses
- Saginaw Bay
- Sauble Beach
- Shipwrecks of the 1913 Great Lakes storm and List of victims of the 1913 Great Lakes storm
- Thunder Bay
- Wasaga Beach

Lake Huron viewed from Arch Rock at Mackinac Island

Great Lakes in general

- Great Lakes
- Great Lakes Areas of Concern
- Great Lakes census statistical areas
- Great Lakes Commission
- Great Recycling and Northern Development Canal
- Great Storm of 1913
- International Boundary Waters Treaty
- List of cities along the Great Lakes
- Seiche
- Sixty Years' War for control of the Great Lakes
- Third Coast

External links

- EPA's Great Lakes Atlas [1]
- Fish Species of Lake Huron [2]
- Great Lakes Coast Watch [3]
- Lake Huron Binational Partnership Action Plan [4]
- Lake Huron Data [5]
- Lake Huron GIS [6]
- Michigan DNR map of Lake Huron [7]

- Bathymetry of Lake Huron [8]

Lighthouses

- Interactive map of lighthouses, Georgian Bay, Lake Huron [9]
- Interactive map of lighthouses in North and East Lake Huron [10]
- Interactive map of lighthouses in North and West Lake Huron [11]

Dow Event Center

"The Dow"	
Location	303 Johnson Street Saginaw, MI 48607-1213
Opened	1972
Owner	City of Saginaw
Capacity	Hockey 5,497 Arena Football 5,201
Tenants	
Saginaw Spirit (OHL) (2002-present) Saginaw Sting (UIFL) (2008-2009, 2011-future)	

The Dow Event Center (formerly known as **The Saginaw County Event Center**, formerly known as The **Saginaw Civic Center**) is located in downtown Saginaw, Michigan. The center consists of three parts: **Heritage Theater**, a meeting facility formerly known as **Unity Hall**, and **Wendler Arena**, an ice rink. It also houses the OHL junior ice hockey team named Saginaw Spirit. In 2008 served its first year as host to the Indoor Football League's now defunct Saginaw Sting. The facility has housed a number of hockey teams in the past, such as the Saginaw LumberKings, Saginaw Wheels and both the IHL and UHL incarnations of the Saginaw Gears.

Wendler Arena has a capacity of 7,600 people for concerts (without the ice), and 5,500 for hockey games. Heritage Theater has a capacity of 2,276 people.

Pregame Warm-up at Wendler Arena.

Originally built in 1972 as part of an urban development program, the center is the only existing structure left. Most of the other buildings were razed in the 1980s due to many problems, including health risks and foreclosure/bankruptcy.

For a time in the 1990s, the facility nearly faced foreclosure and bankruptcy due to lack of funds provided by the city. The facility underwent a series of much-needed renovations in early 2000s, mainly in hopes for a better facility to host their newly-acquired hockey team. The naming rights of the facility were transferred in September 2004 to The Dow Chemical Company [1], headquartered in nearby Midland. The center was used two times during the summer of 2004 as a center for Republican political rallies in support for the re-election of U.S. President George W. Bush.

Voters transferred the ownership from the City of Saginaw to Saginaw County on May 8, 2001. The city then closed the facility on June 30, 2001, and the county reopened it on July 1. The county then appointed SMG Worldwide to manage the facility, and started updating and renovating the building.

The total cost of the renovations was tagged at $17 million, and they were completed in 2003.

Currently, the center houses the Spirit, and hosts many events, concerts, political rallies, and even graduations. Trade shows also take place here; the complex has 25000 square feet (2300 m^2) of space at Wendler Arena.

It hosted the third WWF In Your House pay-per-view on September 24, 1995.

Jehovah's Witnesses District Conventions are held annually at the Dow Event Center. Starting in mid-June, and ending in early July, 3 day conventions held on every weekend in that time will occur. The Jehovah's Witnesses first started using the building in 2005, after rumors of demolition for the Pontiac Silverdome raised concern over where meetings would be held, as the Silverdome was the previous venue.

External links

- The Dow Event Center site [2]
- Dow announcement to purchase naming rights [1]
- Dow Event Center press release on naming rights [3]
- Dow Event Center History [4]
- SMG Worldwide Management Group [5]

Geographical coordinates: 43°26'09.50"N 83°56'12.80"W

Saginaw Spirit

Saginaw Spirit	
City	Saginaw, Michigan
League	Ontario Hockey League
Conference	Western
Division	West
Founded	2002–03
Home arena	The Dow Event Center
Colours	Midnight blue, red, silver, white and yellow
General manager	Todd Watson
Head coach	Todd Watson
Affiliate(s)	Leamington Flyers
Website www.saginawspirit.com [1]	
Franchise history	
1943–47	St. Catharines Falcons
1947–62	St. Catharines Teepees
1962–76	St. Catharines Black Hawks
1976–82	Niagara Falls Flyers
1982–02	North Bay Centennials
2002–	Saginaw Spirit

The **Saginaw Spirit** is a junior ice hockey team based in Saginaw, Michigan. They are members of the West Division of the Western Conference of the Ontario Hockey League (OHL), one of the leagues of the Canadian Hockey League (CHL).

Saginaw Spirit

History

The Saginaw Spirit were born when Dick Garber, the owner of several local automobile dealerships, purchased the North Bay Centennials and moved the team to Saginaw after the 2001–02 season, renaming it the Saginaw Spirit.

The team traces its roots back to St. Catharines, Ontario, where it played as the Falcons, Teepees, and Black Hawks from 1943–1976. It won two Memorial Cup championships as the Teepees, in 1954 and 1960. In 1976, the franchise moved to nearby Niagara Falls, where it was known as the Flyers. In 1982, the team was moved again, this time to North Bay, and renamed the Centennials, where it remained until moving to Saginaw in 2002.

The Spirit have done extensive promotions in the Mid-Michigan area, increasing their fan base and season ticket-holder numbers. The Spirit have one of the highest attendance rates in the Ontario Hockey League.[*citation needed*]

After three rebuilding seasons the Spirit clinched their first playoff berth on March 2, 2006, but lost in the first round to the Guelph Storm. They made the playoffs the following two seasons, but lost to the division rival Sault Ste. Marie Greyhounds both times, in six games in 2007 and in four games in 2008. In 2009, the Spirit won their first playoff series since relocating to Saginaw, sweeping Guelph in four games. They were then swept in the second round by the London Knights.

Coaches

The first coach in Saginaw Spirit history was Dennis Desrosiers. He was well known to local fans, with many years of hockey experience in Michigan. As a player he spent 10 years for the Saginaw Gears (IHL), and spent time coaching the Flint Generals, Saginaw Generals & Kalamazoo Wings all in Michigan. In total, there have been four coaches in Saginaw Spirit history to date

List of coaches. Numbers of seasons in parentheses.

- **2002–03** - Dennis Desrosiers (2)
- **2003–04** - Dennis Desrosiers / Moe Mantha
- **2004–05** - Doug Lidster / Bob Mancini
- **2005–07** - Bob Mancini (3)
- **2007–present** - Todd Watson

Players

See complete list of all **List of Saginaw Spirit alumni**.

Award winners

- *2003–04* - **Patrick McNeill**, Jack Ferguson Award -1st overall OHL Priority Draft Selection
- *2005–06* - **Ryan Daniels**, F.W. "Dinty" Moore Trophy -Best Rookie GAA
- *2005–06* - **Craig Goslin**, OHL Executive of the Year
- *2006–07* - **Tom Pyatt**, William Hanley Trophy -Most Sportsmanlike Player of the Year
- *2006–07* - **Craig Goslin**, OHL Executive of the Year

NHL alumni

Since 2002 the Saginaw Spirit have graduated eight players who have played in the National Hockey League.

- Cody Bass
- T. J. Brodie
- Paul Bissonnette
- Matt Corrente
- Ryan O'Marra
- Geoff Platt
- Tom Pyatt
- Chris Thorburn

Current squad

Roster updated as of October 8, 2010

		Goaltenders				
Number		**Player**	**Glove**	**Acquired**	**NHL Draft**	**Place of birth**
1		Tadeas Galansky	L	Saginaw Spirit 2009	Undrafted	Czech Republic
49		O/A Mavric Parks	L	Trade **BAR** 2010	Undrafted	Eganville, Ontario
57		Jake Paterson	L	Saginaw Spirit 2010	2012	Mississauga, Ontario
		Defensemen				
Number		**Player**	**Shoots**	**Acquired**	**NHL Draft**	**Place of birth**
2		Brad Walch	L	Saginaw Spirit 2007	Undrafted	Saginaw, Michigan
7		O/A Matt Ashman - A	R	Trade **LDN** 2010	Undrafted	London, Ontario
14		Alex Lepkowski	L	Saginaw Spirit 2009	2011	West Seneca, New York
17		O/A Joe Underwood (injured)	R	Trade **GUE** 2007	Undrafted	Canton, Michigan
21		Ryan O'Connor - A (injured)	R	Trade **BAR** 2009	Undrafted	Hamilton, Ontario

27		Frank Schumacher	L	Saginaw Spirit 2009	2012	Brighton, Michigan
71		Peter Hermengildo	R	Trade SUD 2009	Undrafted	Thornhill, Ontario
77		Dalton Young	L	Free Agent 2010	2011	Marysville, Michigan
79		Jacub Ringuette	L	Saginaw Spirit 2010	2012	Goderich, Ontario

Forwards							
Number		Player	Shoots	Position	Acquired	NHL Draft	Place of birth
5		Garrett Ross	L	LW	Free Agent 2009	Undrafted	Dearborn, Michigan
9		Justin Kea	L	C	Saginaw Spirit 2010	2012	Woodville, Ontario
11		Alex Racino	L	C	Free Agent 2010	2011	Merrill, Wisconsin
14		Jordan Szwarz - C	R	RW	Saginaw Spirit 2007	PHX 2009	Burlington, Ontario
15		Anthony Camara	L	LW	Saginaw Spirit 2009	2011	Toronto, Ontario
16		Terry Trafford	L	C	Saginaw Spirit 2010	2012	Toronto, Ontario
19		Michael Kantor	R	RW	Free Agent 2010	Undrafted	Lake Forest, Illinois
20		O/A Mitch Fillman (home, awaiting trade)	R	RW	Free Agent 2007	Undrafted	Oakville, Ontario
22		Brandon Saad	R	C	Saginaw Spirit 2008	2011	Gibsonia, Pennsylvania
24		Ivan Telegin	L	C	Saginaw Spirit 2009	ATL 2010	Novokuznetsk, Russia
25		Josh Shalla	L	LW	Trade GUE 2009	Undrafted	Whitby, Ontario
44		Mickey Sartoretto	R	RW	Traded KIT 2010	Undrafted	Sault Ste. Marie, Ontario
67		O/A Barry Sanderson (home, awaiting trade)	R	C	Trade NIA 2008	Undrafted	Dearborn, Michigan
89		Vincent Trocheck	R	C	Saginaw Spirit 2009	2011	Pittsburgh, Pennsylvania
93		Michael Sgarbossa	L	C	Trade BAR 2009	Undrafted †	Campbellville, Ontario

† Michael Sgarbossa's NHL rights are held by the San Jose Sharks via free agency.

Team records

Team records for a single season		
Statistic	Total	Season
Most points	91	2006–07
Most wins	44	2006–07
Most goals for	291	2006–07
Least goals for	150	2004–05
Least goals against	217	2006–07
Most goals against	275	2002–03

Individual player records for a single season			
Statistic	Player	Total	Season
Most goals	Ryan McDonough	45	2007–08
Most assists	Jordan Skellett	62	2009–10
Most points	Jack Combs	100	2007–08
Most points, rookie	Jan Mursak	80	2006–07
Most points, defenseman	Patrick McNeill	77	2006–07
Best GAA, goalie	Ryan Daniels	2.94	2006–07
Goalies = minimum 1500 minutes played			

Season-by-season results

Regular season

Legend: OTL = Overtime loss, SL = Shootout loss

Season	Games	Won	Lost	Tied	OTL	SL	Points	Pct %	Goals For	Goals Against	Standing
2002–03	68	11	45	5	7	–	34	0.250	158	275	5th West
2003–04	68	16	45	3	4	–	39	0.287	161	228	5th West
2004–05	68	18	42	4	4	–	44	0.324	150	260	4th West
2005–06	68	36	30	–	2	0	74	0.544	242	246	2nd West
2006–07	68	44	21	–	0	3	91	0.669	291	217	2nd West
2007–08	68	33	25	–	8	2	76	0.559	234	231	4th West
2008–09	68	36	24	–	4	4	80	0.588	235	219	2nd West
2009–10	68	34	27	–	4	3	75	0.551	240	230	4th West

Playoffs

- **2002–03** Out of playoffs.
- **2003–04** Out of playoffs.
- **2004–05** Out of playoffs.
- **2005–06** Lost to Guelph Storm 4 games to 0 in conference quarter-finals.
- **2006–07** Lost to Sault Ste. Marie Greyhounds 4 games to 2 in conference quarter-finals.
- **2007–08** Lost to Sault Ste. Marie Greyhounds 4 games to 0 in conference quarter-finals.
- **2008–09** Defeated Guelph Storm 4 games to 0 in conference quarter-finals.
  Lost to London Knights 4 games to 0 in conference semi-finals.
- **2009–10** Lost to Kitchener Rangers 4 games to 2 in conference quarter-finals.

Uniforms and logos

The Saginaw Spirit logo depicts an American bald eagle with the colors of the Stars and Stripes along its neck, on the words "Saginaw Spirit." The uniform scheme is similar to that previously used by the U.S.A. national team. The home jerseys are white backgrounds with navy blue sleeves and red trim. The away jerseys are navy blue backgrounds with red sleeves and white trim. The Saginaw third jersey has a red background with navy blue sleeves and white trim, bearing across the chest the word "Saginaw" spelled diagonally downwards from left to right.

Mascots

Saginaw's main mascot is "Sammy Spirit," resembling an American bald eagle. The team held a vote on their website to name a new secondary mascot for the 2006–07 season. The mascot was named *Steagle Colbeagle the Eagle* after Stephen Colbert. Colbert had promoted the contest on his show, *The Colbert Report*. After naming the mascot after Colbert, the Spirit won seven straight games before losing to the Sarnia Sting on October 20. Since then, *The Colbert Report* has featured ongoing comedy sketches related to the team, the mascot, and other teams in the Ontario Hockey League, especially the Oshawa Generals, and Oshawa, Ontario mayor John Gray.

Arena

The Spirit play at Wendler Arena (capacity 5,527), which is part of The Dow Event Center complex in downtown Saginaw. The **OHL All-Star Classic** was hosted here in 2007. This was the first time in history that the OHL All-Star Game was hosted in an American city. The Arena was formerly home to the Saginaw Gears, Saginaw Generals, Saginaw Hawks, Saginaw Wheels and the Saginaw Lumber Kings.

Capacity = 5,527

Ice size = 192' x 85'

- **Wendler Arena** [2] The OHL Arena & Travel Guide

Mid Michigan Spirit

The Saginaw Spirit in partnership with Meijer food stores sponsor the Mid Michigan Spirit, a women's hockey club based in Midland, Michigan. The 16U team took second at the MAHA state tournament during the 2006-2007 season. A 16U team moved up to 19U for the 2007-2008 season and once again took second at the MAHA state tournament in Canton, Michigan on March 9, 2008.

External links

- www.saginawspirit.com [1] Saginaw Spirit official site
- Ontario Hockey League [3] Official web site
- Canadian Hockey League [4] Official web site

Saginaw Sting

Saginaw Sting	
Founded	2008
League	CIFL 2008 IFL 2009 UIFL 2011-Present
Team history	Saginaw Sting 2008-2009 2011-Present
Arena	Dow Event Center
Based in	Saginaw, Michigan
Team colors	green, orange
Owner	Tony Stewart Andre White
President	Tony Stewart Andre White
Head coach	Ervin Bryson
Championships	2008 CIFL Champions
Division titles	2008 CIFL Atlantic Division
Dancers	Stingers
Mascot	Stanley Stinger

The **Saginaw Sting** are a team in the Ultimate Indoor Football League that began play as a 2008 expansion franchise in the Continental Indoor Football League and then moved to the Indoor Football League for the 2009 season and then folded after the season. The team plays its home games at The Dow Event Center in Saginaw, Michigan.

On June 29, 2008, the Sting defeated the Xplosion 41-37 to win the CIFL Championship Game.

History

Original Team owners are Mike Johnson, Mike Trumbull and Esteban Rivera who also own the Kalamazoo Xplosion. A number of Sting players and Xplosion players indicated at the end of the 2008 season that wages was in arrears from the owners. this lead to an investigation of Johnson in his roll as Sting General Manager. Trumbull, owner of Triple Threat Sports in Battle Creek, and Rivera, a Battle

Creek police officer, have offered a deal to split ownership of the two team with Trumbell and Rivera owning the Sting and Johnson receiving the Xplosion. Trumbull and Rivera has indicated that they plan for the Sting to move to the new Indoor Football League.

Season-By-Season

Note: W = Wins, L = Losses, T = Ties

Season	W	L	T	Finish	Playoff results
Saginaw Sting (CIFL)					
2008	10	2	0	2nd Atlantic West	Won AD West Finals (Marion) Won AD Championship (Lehigh Valley) **Won CIFL Championship (Kalamazoo)**
Saginaw Sting (IFL)					
2009	3	12	0	4th United Atlantic	--
Totals	16	14	0	(including playoffs)	

2009 season schedule

Date	Opponent	Home/Away	Result
March 13	Muskegon Thunder	Away	Won 16-9
March 20	RiverCity Rage	Home	
March 29	Rochester Raiders	Home	
April 4	RiverCity Rage	Away	
April 10	Muskegon Thunder	Home	
April 18	Bloomington Extreme	Away	
April 25	RiverCity Rage	Away	
May 1	Muskegon Thunder	Away	
May 8	Maryland Maniacs	Home	
May 16	Maryland Maniacs	Away	
May 22	Bloomington Extreme	Home	
May 30	Rochester Raiders	Away	
June 5	Maryland Maniacs	Home	
June 19	Sioux City Bandits	Home	

References

External links

- Official Saginaw Sting Website [1]

2008 Season Schedule

Date	Opponent	Home/Away	Result
March 9	Flint Phantoms	Away	Won 51-25
March 21	Marion Mayhem	Home	Won 54-48
March 29	Miami Valley Silverbacks	Away	Won 70-26
April 4	New Jersey Revolution	Home	Won 48-24
April 11	Flint Phantoms	Home	Won 55-28
April 19	Rochester Raiders	Away	Lost 43-59
April 26	Rock River Raptors	Away	Lost 50-51
May 2	Milwaukee Bonecrushers	Home	Won 51-28
May 10	Fort Wayne Freedom	Away	Won 34-21
May 24	Chicago Slaughter	Home	Won 53-28
May 31	Milwaukee Bonecrushers	Away	Won 54-28
June 6	Muskegon Thunder	Home	Won 60-23
Playoff			
June 14	Marion Mayhem (Playoffs)	Home	Won 41-34
June 23	Lehigh Valley Outlawz (Playoffs)	Home	Won 59-25
June 29	Kalamazoo Xplosion (CIFL Championship)	Away	Won 41-37

Transportation

MBS International Airport

MBS International Airport	
IATA: MBS – ICAO: KMBS – FAA LID: MBS	
Summary	
Airport type	Public
Owner	MBS International
Serves	Saginaw, Michigan Midland, Michigan Bay City, Michigan
Location	Tittabawassee Township, Saginaw County, Michigan
Hub for	{{{hub}}}
Elevation AMSL	668 ft / 204 m
Coordinates	43°31′58″N 084°04′47″W
Runways	

Direction	Length		Surface
	ft	m	
5/23	8,002	2,439	Asphalt
14/32	6,400	1,951	Asphalt

Statistics (2006)	
Aircraft operations	50,254
Based aircraft	27
Source: Federal Aviation Administration	

MBS International Airport (IATA: **MBS**, ICAO: **KMBS**, FAA LID: **MBS**) is located in Freeland, Michigan, serving the nearby cities of Midland, Bay City, and Saginaw. It was formerly named **Tri City Airport** or **Freeland Tri-City Airport**. The airport was renamed to MBS International Airport in 1994 (representative of its IATA airport code) to prevent confusion with other airports named "Tri City Airport" across the United States.

The commercial airport is a special municipal body owned by Bay County and the cities of Midland and Saginaw. The airports's name is an initialism formed from the names of the three owning communities. It is governed by a nine-member commission made up of three members from each of the owning communities.

Facilities

MBS International Airport covers 3,200 acres (13 km²) and has two runways:

- Runway 5/23: 8,002 x 150 ft (2,439 x 46 m), Surface: Asphalt
- Runway 14/32: 6,400 x 150 ft (1,951 x 46 m), Surface: Asphalt

History

During World War II, it was used to hold prisoners of war. Civilian control of the airport resumed in the mid 1940s.

The 1980s and 1990s saw a lot of growth at MBS. During this time, airline service expanded and many airlines began serving MBS.

- During the 1980s, Air Canada operated the Jetstream 31, linking MBS with Toronto, Canada.
- American Eagle Airlines operated Shorts 360 turboprop aircraft between MBS and Chicago, Illinois, as well as Lansing, Grand Rapids, Kalamazoo, and Traverse City. American left MBS in the late 1980s.
- Chicago Express Airlines, the now-defunct ATA Airlines carrier, served MBS in the early 1990s with daily service to Chicago Midway Airport using the Jetstream 31 turboprop aircraft.
- Comair (Delta Connection) briefly linked MBS with Cincinnati, Ohio, using Embraer EMB 120 Brasilia, a 32-seat turboprop. Comair left MBS and started service in Flint, where they terminated service years later.
- Continental Airlines provided mainline service in the 1980s to Cleveland, Ohio. The airline used McDonnell Douglas DC-9 and Boeing 737 aircraft on this route. Mainline service was downgraded to Continental Express service in the late 1980s. Continental Express used Beechcraft 1900 turboprop aircraft. Service to Flint and Chicago Midway also existed in 1992. The airline left MBS in the mid-1990s and returned in 2002. Service was dropped to Cleveland again in 2003.
- Republic Airlines served MBS in the 1960s, 1970s, and 1980s. The airline linked MBS with Detroit using the DC-9 aircraft. During this time, Republic Express provided turboprop service to Flint, Grand Rapids, and Traverse City. Republic stopped MBS service when they merged with Northwest Airlines in the 1980s, and in 2010, Northwest merged with Delta Air Lines. Delta still serves MBS today.
- Skyway Airlines (The Midwest Express Connection) served MBS in the 1990s with service to Milwaukee, Wisconsin, using the Beechcraft 1900 turboprop aircraft. Skyway also tried service to

Toronto, Flint, and Grand Rapids in the late 1990s. The airline pulled out in the late 1990s.
- United Airlines provided MBS with mainline service since commercial service was started. In the 1980s and 1990s, United linked MBS with Chicago using Boeing 737 and 727 aircraft. Service to Denver, Colorado, also existed in the 1980s. Mainline United left MBS in the late 1990s, and was replaced with United Express, which still serves MBS with service to Chicago's O'Hare International Airport using the 50 seat Bombardier Canadair Regional Jet (CRJ) aircraft.
- US Airways began service to MBS in 1996, operating Fokker 100 and Boeing 737 aircraft to Pittsburgh, Pennsylvania. Mainline service ended soon after, and US Airways Express assumed the Pittsburgh flights using the Beech 1900 and Saab 340 aircraft. US Airways suspended service to MBS just two days after entering Chapter 11 bankruptcy protection in late 2002. At the time it was the only city for US Airways to drop. Since then, US Airways has also left Flint, Lansing, Kalamazoo, and Grand Rapids, leaving Detroit as the only Michigan destination served by US Airways.
- Air Force One landed at the airport two times during the 2004 United States Election for nearby rallies in support of George W. Bush (Air Force One also visited the airport in 1974 when then President Richard M. Nixon made a speech at the airport and arrived to give endorsement to James Sparling, a Congressional candidate).

Current operations

Once the third busiest airport in Michigan, MBS has fallen in air service and passenger numbers. One major reason for this is the low-cost competition at nearby Bishop International Airport in Flint, which offers more flights to more destinations and often cheaper fares.[citation needed]

2006 enplanements were 200,150 boardings, a 6.33% drop from the previous year.

Air Wisconsin runs ground services for United Express.

Delta Air Lines merged with Northwest Airlines.

Until October 1, 2009 Mesaba Airlines ran ground services for Delta Connection.

Compass Airlines, Comair, and Mesaba Airlines ground handling merged into one service called Regional Elite Airline Services. Regional Elite is 100% owned by Delta Air Lines.

Regional Elite runs ground services for Delta and Delta Connection at MBS.

New Terminal

In early 2007, it was announced that the Airport Commission has approved plans for the construction of a new state-of-the-art passenger terminal. This new $48-million, 75000 sq ft (7000 m^2) project would begin sometime in 2007 and will take 18 months. The new terminal will be built just north of the current terminal. Airport officials hope this will bring more airlines and more competition to MBS.

Airlines

Airlines	Destinations
Delta Connection operated by Pinnacle Airlines	Detroit, Minneapolis/St. Paul
United Express operated by SkyWest Airlines	Chicago-O'Hare
United Express operated by Mesa Airlines	Chicago-O'Hare

Accidents and incidents

- On 6 April 1958, Vickers Viscount N7437, operating Capital Airlines Flight 67, stalled and crashed on approach. All 47 on board were killed. The cause was attributed to ice accretion on the horizontal stabiliser.
- On August 16, 1987 a Northwest Airlines MD-80, Northwest Airlines Flight 255, originated at MBS. After departing MBS, the flight dropped off and picked up passengers at Detroit Metropolitan Wayne County Airport before crashing on takeoff en route to Phoenix, Arizona, killing 148 passengers and 6 crew members.

See also

- Michigan World War II Army Airfields

References

This article incorporates public domain material from websites or documents [1] *of the Air Force Historical Research Agency.*

External links

- MBS International Airport [1] (official site)
- Michigan Bureau of Aeronautics [2]
- Resources for this airport:
    - AirNav airport information for KMBS [3]
    - ASN accident history for MBS [4]
    - FlightAware airport information [5] and live flight tracker [6]
    - NOAA/NWS latest weather observations [7]
    - SkyVector aeronautical chart for KMBS [8]
    - FAA current MBS delay information [9]

Bishop International Airport

Bishop International Airport	
IATA: FNT – ICAO: KFNT	
Summary	
Airport type	Public
Operator	Bishop International Airport Authority
Serves	Flint, Michigan
Hub for	{{{hub}}}
Elevation AMSL	782 ft / 238.4 m
Coordinates	42°57′56″N 083°44′37″W
Website	www.bishopairport.org [1]

Runways			
Direction	Length		Surface
	ft	m	
18/36	7,848	2,392	Asphalt
9/27	7,200	2,195	Asphalt

Bishop International Airport (IATA: **FNT**, ICAO: **KFNT**) is an airport located in the city of Flint, Michigan. The third busiest airport in Michigan, it surpassed competitor MBS International Airport in terms of airline operations in 2002. In 2007, 1,072,420 passengers used Bishop Airport, followed by a slight drop to 1,050,813 passengers in 2008. There are currently six commercial airlines flying into and out of Flint today. It is also served by numerous cargo operators. Accompanying the airlines is a fixed base operator that handles both general aviation and airline operations and one flight school.

Facilities

Bishop International Airport covers 1,550 acres (6 km²) and has two runways.

- Runway 18/36: 7,848 x 150 ft. (2,392 x 46 m), Surface: Asphalt/Concrete
- Runway 9/27: 7,200 x 150 ft. (2,195 x 46 m), Surface: Asphalt

Airlines and destinations

Airlines	Destinations
AirTran Airways	Atlanta, Fort Lauderdale [seasonal], Fort Myers [seasonal], Orlando, Tampa
AmericanConnection operated by Chautauqua Airlines	Chicago-O'Hare
Continental Connection operated by CommutAir	Cleveland
Delta Air Lines	Atlanta
Delta Connection operated by Atlantic Southeast Airlines	Atlanta
Delta Connection operated by Mesaba Airlines	Detroit
Delta Connection operated by Pinnacle Airlines	Detroit, Minneapolis/St. Paul
Midwest Connect operated by Chautauqua Airlines	Milwaukee

Recent history

Air traffic and passenger numbers at Bishop International have grown since AirTran started service in the early 2000s. At a time when passenger numbers dropped around the US, Flint's Bishop Airport was one of only a few airports to show growth.[citation needed] Passengers from the Detroit area were choosing Flint because of low fares and conveniences including short check-in and security lines and a hassle-free terminal building. [citation needed] In 2002, Flint bypassed MBS International Airport in Saginaw, Michigan to carrying more passengers to more destinations. [citation needed] Flint has also gone over some recent baggage claim extensions adding two more carousels bringing the total number to four.

Today, there is a great variety of airlines that fly their aircraft to many destinations from Flint. As a result of the popularity of some Flint-based routes, competition has been sparked among airlines. AirTran and Northwest Airlines are two great examples. In 2005, AirTran announced service to Fort Myers. A day later, Northwest announced the same service.[citation needed] Two days after Northwest's announcement, AirTran also announced nonstop flights from Flint to Las Vegas service starting a day before Northwest's planned start, and a 20-minute earlier departure. [citation needed] AirTran discontinued nonstop service to Las Vegas June 24, 2008, blaming the high price of jet fuel.

In 2005 and 2006, Flint resumed operation to Chicago O'Hare on American Eagle. In September 2007, American Eagle added a non-stop flight to Dallas Fort Worth. In November 2007, a non-stop flight to New York's LaGuardia airport was added by both American Eagle and Northwest Airlink, a subsidiary of Northwest Airlines. American Eagle stopped the flight to LaGuardia April 1, 2008. In February 2009, Northwest Airlines transferred the daily nonstop Northwest Airlink flight to nearby MBS International Airport.

In early February 2007, Bishop Airport unveiled a comprehensive 5-year developmental plan that would be slated for continuation through late 2011. The program called for two phases of "Intermodal Facility Development," including the expansion of the West Cargo Apron, what is now known as the Abex and Emory GVA Freight Ramp, located on the airport's northwest side.

The year 2008 was scheduled to include the design of a terminal ramp upgrade and the design of concourse area improvements including the recently-announced addition of free airport-wide wireless internet access. Both projects are scheduled to begin in 2009.

In May 2009, Bishop Airport began Phase I of its Terminal Airside & Concourse Improvements program. Projects under this phase were developed in 2008. Included in this phase are upgrades to the terminal ramp, upon which the passenger concourse resides; the permanent closure and deconstruction of Runway 5/23; and the acquisition of new land for an envisioned Runway 9L/27R, which is scheduled to be designed in 2009 and constructed in 2010.

Runway 5/23 was closed permanently on May 4, 2009 as progress continued in the Capital Improvement Program. An additional runway, Runway 9R/27L, is scheduled for completion in 2010 under the same program.

The Airport's Future

According to an internal improvement assessment included in the FNT Airport Capital Improvement Program projects approximately 750,000 passenger enplanements within the next 6 to 10 years, shadowed by the current statistic of approximately 600,000 annual passenger enplanements. The airport's 5-year improvement plan is calling for an additional runway, enhancements to the economy parking lot, and improvements to general aviation facilities.

Ground transportation

Bishop International Airport is accessible from I-69, I-75, and US 23 by exiting Bristol road. The airport is also served by a bus line operated by the Flint MTA. The airport has car rental spots also.

Cargo Operations

In addition to airline operations, Flint's Bishop International Airport is also becoming a notable player in the air cargo industry. With nearby connections to two major interstates and one U.S. highway, in addition to numerous rail lines, a cargo hub is in development at Bishop Airport that is predicted to become a major benefit to the Flint-area economy.

The Flint-Bishop Airport is served by major cargo operators including FedEx Express. Milwaukee-based Skyway Airlines began cargo operations out of Flint in early 2008, adding to the list of cargo operators at Bishop Airport.

External links

- Bishop International Airport [1] - Official website
- Resources for this airport:
    - AirNav airport information for KFNT [2]
    - ASN accident history for FNT [3]
    - FlightAware airport information [4] and live flight tracker [5]
    - NOAA/NWS latest weather observations [6]
    - SkyVector aeronautical chart for KFNT [7]
    - FAA current FNT delay information [8]
- AvFlight Flint [9] - Fixed Base Operator
- American Wings Aviation [10] - Flight School

Interstate 75

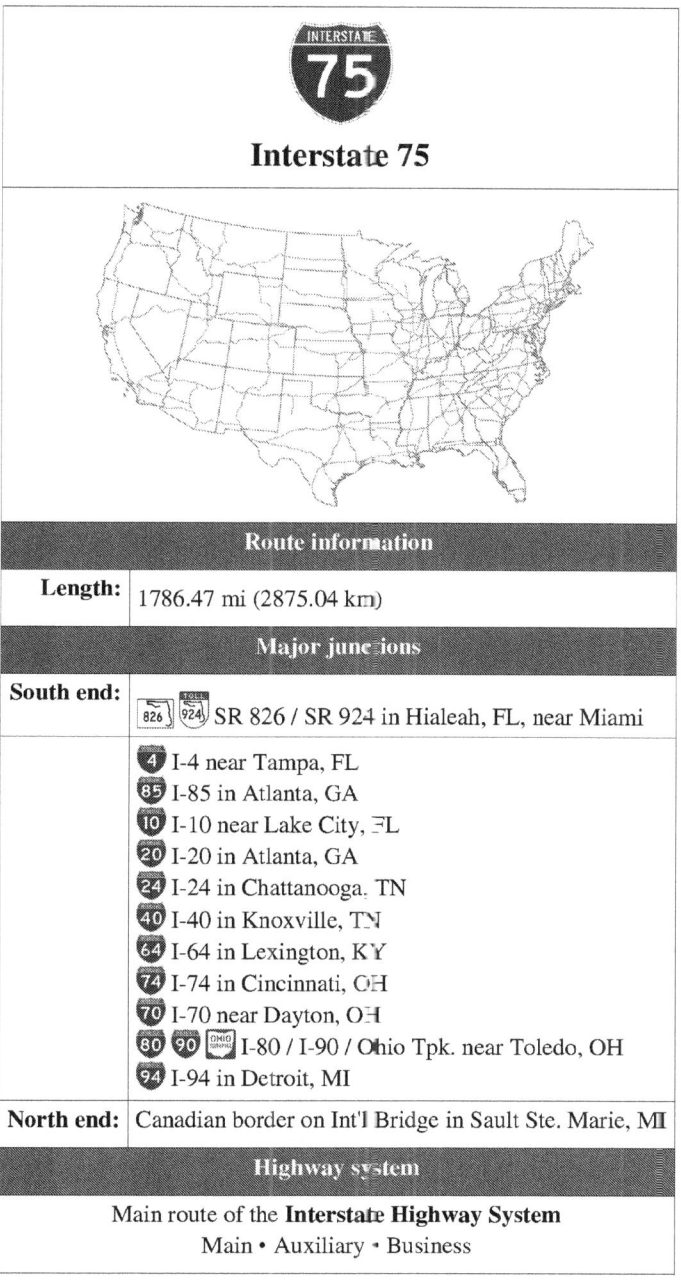

Interstate 75	
Route information	
Length:	1786.47 mi (2875.04 km)
Major junctions	
South end:	SR 826 / SR 924 in Hialeah, FL, near Miami
	I-4 near Tampa, FL
	I-85 in Atlanta, GA
	I-10 near Lake City, FL
	I-20 in Atlanta, GA
	I-24 in Chattanooga, TN
	I-40 in Knoxville, TN
	I-64 in Lexington, KY
	I-74 in Cincinnati, OH
	I-70 near Dayton, OH
	I-80 / I-90 / Ohio Tpk. near Toledo, OH
	I-94 in Detroit, MI
North end:	Canadian border on Int'l Bridge in Sault Ste. Marie, MI
Highway system	
Main route of the **Interstate Highway System** Main • Auxiliary • Business	

Interstate 75 (**I-75**) is a major north–south Interstate Highway in the Great Lakes and Southeastern regions of the United States. It travels from State Road 826 (Palmetto Expressway) and State Road 924

(Gratigny Parkway) in Hialeah, Florida (northwest of Miami) to Sault Ste. Marie, Michigan, at the Ontario, Canada, border. Interstate 75 passes through six different states: Florida, Georgia, Tennessee, Kentucky, Ohio and Michigan.

Route description

Lengths

	mi	km
FL	470.88	757.81
GA	355.11	571.49
TN	161.86	260.49
KY	191.78	308.64
OH	211.30	340.05
MI	395.54	636.56
Total	1786.47	2875.04

Florida

Main article: Interstate 75 in Florida

Interstate 75 begins its northerly journey at an interchange with State Road 924 and State Road 826 in Hialeah, a suburb of Miami. After an intersection with the Homestead Extension of Florida's Turnpike and an interchange with Interstate 595 and the Sawgrass Expressway, the interstate leaves the Miami metropolitan area and turns westward to travel through the Everglades along the tolled Alligator Alley, which brings the highway to the Gulf Coast and Naples, where it again heads north. Passing through Bonita Springs, Fort Myers, and Sarasota, Interstate 75 encounters a series of construction projects that will increase the lane count from two lanes in each direction to three in each direction. The freeway enters the Tampa Bay metropolitan area before the interchange with Interstate 275 northbound, which handles St. Petersburg-bound traffic. Within the Tampa metro are three more major junctions: One with the Lee Roy Selmon Crosstown Expressway which carries traffic into downtown Tampa; one with Interstate 4 which carries traffic across the center of the state to the East Coast; and another as Interstate 275 traffic defaults back onto northbound. The freeway proceeds to enter suburban portions of Pasco, Hernando, and Sumter counties on its way to Ocala and Gainesville. At Lake City, Florida, the Christopher Columbus Transcontinental Highway, Interstate 10, intersects with Interstate 75, providing routes toward Jacksonville, Florida; Tallahassee; Mobile, Alabama; and points westward. Afterward, the northmost stetch of Interstate 75 in Florida exits the Sunshine State into southern

Georgia.

Georgia

Main article: Interstate 75 in Georgia

Interstate 75 enters Georgia near Valdosta, and it continues northward through the towns of Tifton and Cordele until it reaches the Macon area, where it intersects with Interstate 16 eastbound towards Savannah. For northbound traffic wishing to avoid potential congestion in Macon, Interstate 475 provides a relatively straight bypass west of that city and Interstate 75's route. After Macon it passes the small town of Forsyth. The freeway reaches no major junctions again until in the Atlanta metropolitan area. The first metropolitan freeway met is Interstate 675, then followed by the Atlanta "Perimeter" bypass, Interstate 285. It crosses inside the Perimeter and heads northeast several miles towards the Atlanta city center. Interstate 75 is then duplexed with Interstate 85 due north through the central business district of Atlanta. After the two Interstates split, Interstate 75 makes a beeline northwest, crossing outside the Interstate 285 Perimeter and heading towards the major suburban city of Marietta. This section of Interstate 75 just north of Interstate 285 has 15 through lanes, making it the widest roadway anywhere in the Interstate Highway System.. North of Marietta, the final major junction in the Atlanta metropolitan area is the Interstate 575 spur. Interstate 75 then traverses the hilly northwestern Georgia terrain as it travels towards Chattanooga, Tennessee.

Tennessee

Main article: Interstate 75 in Tennessee

The freeway enters Tennessee directly in the Chattanooga metropolitan area, where it intersects with Interstate 24. Exiting Chattanooga to the northeast, Interstate 75 passes through an area known for dense fog. Twelve people were killed and 42 were injured in a 99 vehicle accident on that stretch of I-75 in heavy fog on December 11, 1990. Interstate 75 does not meet any other highways until it is multiplexed with Interstate 40 and heads eastbound. Together, they enter the outskirts of Knoxville, where Interstate 75 multiplexes itself with a different road, this time Interstate 640, but only for a short time. When the two meet Interstate 275, Interstate 75 becomes its own freeway and heads north towards the Kentucky border. On the journey northward from Knoxville to the Kentucky border, interstate 75 encounters some of its highest points of elevation through the Cumberland Mountains and Cumberland Plateau region, cutting through the uppermost peaks and ridges of the mountains.

Kentucky

Main article: Interstate 75 in Kentucky

Interstate 75 continues northbound through the hilly and rugged terrain of the Cumberland Plateau region of Kentucky passing through London, KY and Richmond, KY eventually reaching Lexington, where it briefly runs coterminiously with Interstate 64 before splitting off for Cincinnati, Ohio. Near Walton, Interstate 71 merges with Interstate 75, making for yet another multiplexed portion of freeway. Interstate 275, which is the Cincinnati beltway, is then intersected by Interstate 71/75. After passing through Covington, the freeway crosses the Ohio River via the lower level of the Brent Spence Bridge and continues into Cincinnati.

Ohio

Main article: Interstate 75 in Ohio

Immediately after entering Cincinnati, Interstate 71 separates from Interstate 75, taking a more easterly routing through the city, while Interstate 75 remains generally northbound throughout the metropolitan area. Interstate 74 westbound, Ohio State Route 562 eastbound, and Ohio State Route 126 all intersect the freeway as it makes its way northward. In Arlington Heights, a suburb of Cincinnati, Interstate 75 sees a carriageway split for a few miles. After another interchange with the Interstate 275 beltway, the freeway continues in the metropolitan area, passes through Middletown and heads towards Dayton, where Interstate 675 and Interstate 70 have interchanges. After exiting Dayton, Interstate 75 makes its way northbound through Ohio, passing through the smaller cities of Lima, Findlay and Bowling Green before finally reaching Toledo, located on the Michigan border. Interstate 475 is met first south of the city, and then the cross-country highways of Interstate 80/Interstate 90/Ohio Turnpike. Interstate 475 then meets with 75 again. Interstate 280 is the last major junction in Ohio; the freeway crosses into Michigan soon afterwards.

Mackinac Bridge

Michigan

Main article: Interstate 75 in Michigan

Interstate 75 hugs the western shore of Lake Erie upon entering Michigan—until about Monroe, when it heads westward and prepares to enter Detroit and its surrounding suburbs. Yet another I-275 is met as the freeway goes deeper into the Detroit metropolitan area, and no other major junctions are present until downtown. Once downtown, Interstate 75 meets the Ambassador Bridge to Windsor, Ontario, Interstate 375 (Chrysler Freeway), I-94, I-96, M-10 and M-8 (Davison Freeway).

I-696 also intersects I-75 in the northern metro area. When the freeway reaches Pontiac, there is a junction with M-59; and further north in Flint, the interstate meets I-475 and I-69. The freeway then heads north towards Saginaw, where I-675 acts as a spur route into the city. Further north in Bay City, the major junction of US 10 exists, providing access to Midland as well as downtown Bay City. The last major interchange occurs at 4 Mile Road just south of Grayling where US 127 northbound ends with traffic merging onto northbound I-75 and the southbound starts taking drivers through the center of the state granting easier access to cities such as Clare, Mt. Pleasant, Lansing, and Jackson. At Mackinaw City, I-75 crosses the Mackinac Bridge to reach the Upper Peninsula. It is the only Interstate located in the Upper Peninsula of Michigan, and it continues to where the road terminates at the Canadian border in Sault Ste. Marie.

On the Canadian side, drivers must use a series of city streets in Sault Ste. Marie, Ontario to reach Highway 17, the local route of the Trans-Canada Highway.

History

This limited access highway that was planned in the 1950s roughly follows the general route of many older at-grade highways, including U.S. Route 2, U.S. Route 27, U.S. Route 25, and U.S. Route 41, among others. Some of these older U.S. Routes (several of which are still in existence) previously had replaced the eastern route of the old *Dixie Highway*.

Interstate 75 was intended to end at Tampa in the original interstate highway plans. However, vast population growth in southwestern Florida (e.g. Ft. Myers, Naples, etc.) and a desire to link the Tampa Bay Area with South Florida, called for a new expressway artery. At first, Florida state legislators proposed a toll in the corridor, but by 1968, it was cancelled in favor of the extension of I-75 southwards. Next, it was decided to link I-75 from Naples to South Florida with an upgraded version of an existing private toll road, the Alligator Alley, and then connect it with Interstate 95 in North Miami, although due to local opposition, I-75 ends a few miles short of I-95.

On December 21, 1977, I-75 was complete from Tampa to Sault Ste. Marie with a segment opening north of Marietta, Georgia. The final stretch of Interstate 75 was completed in 1986 in Dade (present Miami-Dade) and Broward Counties in Florida, but the last stretch to receive the I-75 signage was a reconstructed (rebuilt with more lanes) Alligator Alley on November 25, 1992.

On July 15, 2009, a fuel tanker exploded under an overpass on 9 Mile Road in Hazel Park resulting in the overpass collapsing onto I-75.

Major intersections

- Homestead Extension of Florida's Turnpike near Miami Lakes, Florida (southbound exit and northbound entrance)
- Interstate 595 in Davie, Florida, serving Fort Lauderdale-Hollywood International Airport
- Interstate 275 near Parrish, Florida
- Florida State Road 60 near Brandon, Florida
- Interstate 4 near Tampa, Florida
- Interstate 275 near Lutz, Florida
- Interstate 10 in Lake City, Florida
- Interstate 475 around Macon, Georgia (twice).
- Interstate 16 in Macon, Georgia (**Map** [1])
- Interstate 675 near Stockbridge, Georgia
- Interstate 285 outside Atlanta (loop around the city), on the southeast side in Clayton County and on the northwest side near Marietta
- Interstate 85 in Atlanta. They stay connected for several miles through downtown on a highway known as the Downtown Connector.
- Interstate 20 in Atlanta
- Interstate 24 in Chattanooga, Tennessee
- Interstate 40 near Lenoir City, Tennessee. They stay connected until Knoxville, Tennessee.
- Interstate 64 in Lexington, Kentucky. They stay connected for 6 miles (9.7 km) to the east of downtown Lexington.
- Interstate 71 in Walton, Kentucky. They stay connected until Cincinnati, Ohio.
- Interstate 275 in Erlanger, Kentucky (loop around Cincinnati), and again in Sharonville, Ohio
- Interstate 74 in Cincinnati
- Interstate 675 in Miamisburg, Ohio (south of Dayton)
- Interstate 70 in Vandalia, Ohio (near Dayton)
- Interstate 80 / 90 (Ohio Turnpike) in Rossford, Ohio (near Toledo)
- Interstate 475 in Perrysburg and Toledo, Ohio
- Interstate 280 in Toledo, Ohio
- Interstate 275 in Newport, Michigan
- Interstate 96 (Jeffries Freeway) in Detroit, Michigan
- M-10 (Lodge Freeway) in Detroit
- Interstate 375 in Detroit
- Interstate 94 (Ford Freeway) in Detroit
- M-8 (Davison Freeway) in Detroit
- Interstate 696 (Walter P. Reuther Freeway) north of Detroit

I-75 co-signed with I-85 in midtown Atlanta

- Interstate 69 in Flint, Michigan
- Interstate 475 in Flint
- Interstate 675 in Saginaw, Michigan
- US 10 west of Bay City, Michigan

Auxiliary routes

- Tampa, Florida/St. Petersburg, Florida - I-175 (1.294 mi/2.08 km), I-275 (63.387 mi/102.01 km), I-375 (1.220 mi/1.96 km)
- Macon, Georgia - I-475
- Atlanta, Georgia - I-675
- Suburban Spur to Canton, Georgia, I-575 in the Atlanta area
- Knoxville, Tennessee - I-275
- Knoxville, Tennessee - I-640
- Cincinnati, Ohio - I-275
- Dayton, Ohio - I-675
- Toledo, Ohio - I-475
- Detroit, Michigan - I-275, I-375
- Flint, Michigan - I-475
- Saginaw, Michigan - I-675

References

- 2005 Rand McNally Road Atlas
- FDOT [1] GIS data and pavement management reports [2]
- Georgia Department of Transportation, Office of Transportation Data (2003). *Interstate Mileage Report (438 Report)* [3].

External links

- Interstate 75 [4] at Michigan Highways
- Interstate 75 [5] on Cincinnati-Transit.net

Interstate 75

Main US Interstate Highways (major interstates highlighted)															
4	5	8	10	12	15	16	17	19	20	22	24	25	26	27	29	30
35	37	39	40	43	44	45	49	55	57	59	64	65	66	68	69	
70	71	72	73	74	75	76 (W)	76 (E)	77	78	79	80	81	82			
83	84 (W)		84 (E)	85	86 (W)		86 (E)	87	88 (W)		88 (E)	89	90			
91	93	94	95	96	97	99	(238)	H-1		H-2		H-3				
Unsigned	A-1		A-2		A-3		A-4		PRI-1		PRI-2		PRI-3			
Lists	**Primary**	Main - Intrastate - Suffixed - Future - Gaps														
	Auxiliary	Main - Future - Unsigned														
	Other	Standards - Business - Bypassed														

Browse numbered routes		
← 74 SR 74	**FL**	SR 75 75 →
← 74 SR 74	**GA**	SR 75 75 →
← 74 KY 74	**KY**	KY 75 75 →
← 74 I-74	**OH**	I-76 76 →
← 74 M-74	**MI**	M-75 75 →

M-47 (Michigan highway)

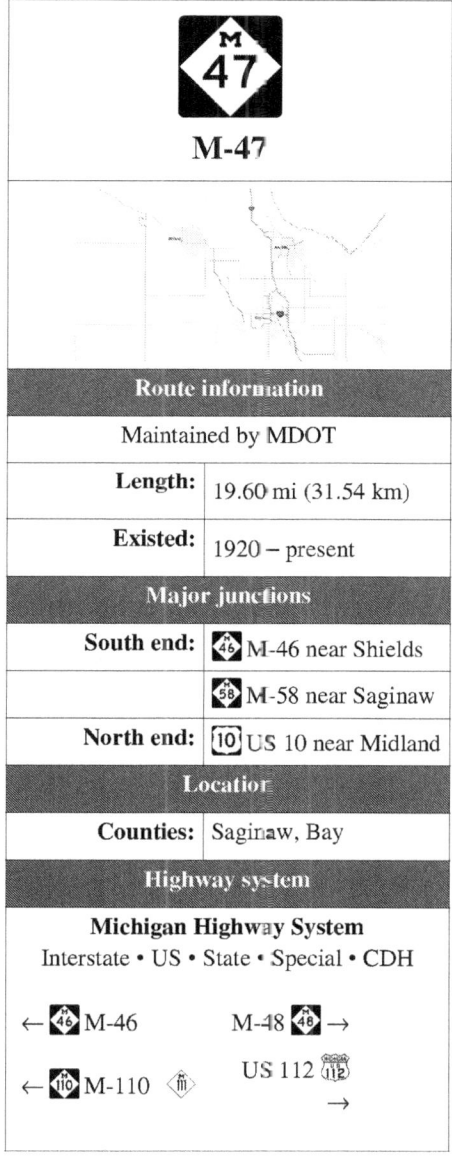

M-47 is a state trunkline in the US state of Michigan. It runs from US 10, just east of Midland to M-46 in Saginaw Charter Township. The routing has changed many times over its history, leaving very little of its original routing intact.

M-47 (Michigan highway)

Route description

M-47 starts at M-46/Gratiot Road east of Shields. M-47 is known as Midland Road as it runs slightly northwest to intersect with M-58/State Road in Saginaw Charter Township running parallel to the Tittabawassee River. At Freeland, M-47 runs near the MBS International Airport off Freeland Road. North of Freeland, M-47 leaves Midland Road to use a freeway segment. Just passed this junction on Midland Road is Tittabawassee Park.

Freeway portion

North of Freeland, the 3 miles (4.8 km) nearest M-47's northern end at US 10 are a limited access highway including interchanges with Salzburg Road and US 10.

History

The history of M-47 begins in 1920. The first designation was routed from the Shiawassee/Ingham county line north to St. Charles and then east along M-46 into Saginaw. The southern extension into Ingham County to end at M-16 in Williamston is transferred and completed 1924. A northern extension to Bay City along today's M-84 was completed in 1930, and extended farther to Bay City State Park in 1933. M-47 would replace M-111 and extend back southerly from the Park to Bay City in 1937, creating a "U-turn" in the routing. The southern terminus was moved again in 1951 to Weberville, still ending on US 16 which had replaced M-16 back in 1926.

Major changes to the routing of M-47 started in 1960. The I-75/US 10/US 23 freeway opened. US 10 is routed east of Midland to Bay City along the M-20 freeway. M-47 is rerouted along the former US 10 from Saginaw to east of Midland. A connector expressway was built from Freeland north to the US 10 freeway. M-81 was extended over State Street in Saginaw, and the former routing of M-47 between Saginaw and Bay City was redesignated as M-84. M-13 also replaces the former US 23/M-47 as US 23 is moved to freeways as well.

The southern end of M-47 was changed in 1962 with the completion of I-96 in the Lansing area. US 16 was replaced by M-43 and the southern terminus was moved to Exit 122 along I-96. This segment of M-47 south of M-46 became an extension of M-52 in 1969. The interchange at Salzburg Road north of Freeland was opened in 1970. The expressway segment is upgraded to a full freeway at this time. The short route of M-47 between its northern terminus and M-46 today stayed intact to eliminate its concurrency on M-46 due to M-52's northern extension to there.[*citation needed*]

M-111

In 1928, **M-111** was assigned to a route connecting M-13 (later signed as US 23 for a time) north of Bay City to Bay City State Park on Saginaw Bay. The original route consisted of what is today Euclid Avenue. In the 1930s, a return leg towards Bay City was added to the east of the original route along what is now State Park Road, giving the route an upside-down U-shape.

In the mid-1930s, the western leg along Euclid Avenue from Midland Road to Beaver Road was designated as M-47. In 1937, all of M-111 was re-designated as M-47—thus making M-47 double back to US 23 about a mile east of a point where it left US 23 after running concurrently with US 23 for two miles (3 km) west of Bay City.

In 1960/1961, the western leg along Euclid Avenue is re-designated as M-247 while the eastern leg along State Park Road is returned to local control.

Major intersections

County	Location	Mile	Destinations	Notes
Saginaw	Shields	0.00	M-46	
	Saginaw Township	1.73	M-58	
		5.49	Tittabawassee Road	
	Freeland	15.22	Midland Road	Freeway begins
Bay	Williams Township	18.60	Salzburg Road	Diamond interchange
	Midland	19.60	US 10	
1.000 mi = 1.609 km; 1.000 km = 0.621 mi				

External links

- M-47 Endpoint Photos [1]

Article Sources and Contributors

Michigan *Source*: http://en.wikipedia.org/?oldid=390673209 *Contributors*: JohnInDC

History of Michigan *Source*: http://en.wikipedia.org/?oldid=386013916 *Contributors*: Allmightyduck

Geography of Michigan *Source*: http://en.wikipedia.org/?oldid=390048243 *Contributors*:

List of Michigan state parks *Source*: http://en.wikipedia.org/?oldid=386373220 *Contributors*: 1 anonymous edits

List of National Historic Landmarks in Michigan *Source*: http://en.wikipedia.org/?oldid=390568986 *Contributors*: Thomas Paine1776

Saginaw, Michigan *Source*: http://en.wikipedia.org/?oldid=389434522 *Contributors*:

Saginaw County, Michigan *Source*: http://en.wikipedia.org/?oldid=384619173 *Contributors*: 1 anonymous edits

Flint/Tri-Cities *Source*: http://en.wikipedia.org/?oldid=389536299 *Contributors*: 1 anonymous edits

History of Saginaw, Michigan *Source*: http://en.wikipedia.org/?oldid=383961603 *Contributors*: Hmains

Temple Theatre (Saginaw, Michigan) *Source*: http://en.wikipedia.org/?oldid=350230812 *Contributors*:

Castle Museum (Saginaw, Michigan) *Source*: http://en.wikipedia.org/?oldid=389875307 *Contributors*:

Fashion Square Mall *Source*: http://en.wikipedia.org/?oldid=386089231 *Contributors*:

Saginaw Trail *Source*: http://en.wikipedia.org/?oldid=385755253 *Contributors*:

Saginaw River *Source*: http://en.wikipedia.org/?oldid=384005687 *Contributors*:

Saginaw Bay *Source*: http://en.wikipedia.org/?oldid=385414854 *Contributors*: Hmains

Lake Huron *Source*: http://en.wikipedia.org/?oldid=386973115 *Contributors*: The High Fin Sperm Whale

Dow Event Center *Source*: http://en.wikipedia.org/?oldid=387961393 *Contributors*: LilHelpa

Saginaw Spirit *Source*: http://en.wikipedia.org/?oldid=389813166 *Contributors*: Kivpit

Saginaw Sting *Source*: http://en.wikipedia.org/?oldid=388048634 *Contributors*:

MBS International Airport *Source*: http://en.wikipedia.org/?oldid=386137166 *Contributors*: Tom Danson

Bishop International Airport *Source*: http://en.wikipedia.org/?oldid=387835916 *Contributors*: 1 anonymous edits

Interstate 75 *Source*: http://en.wikipedia.org/?oldid=387972189 *Contributors*: C.Fred

M-47 (Michigan highway) *Source*: http://en.wikipedia.org/?oldid=381916655 *Contributors*: Imzadi1979

Image Sources, Licenses and Contributors

File:Flag_of_Michigan.svg *Source*: http://en.wikipedia.org/w/index.php?title=File:Flag_of_Michigan.svg *License*: unknown *Contributors*: Awg1010, Denelson83, Dzordzm, Fry1989, Homo lupus, Mattes, Serinde, Svgalbertian, Werewombat, 1 anonymous edits

File:Seal of Michigan.svg *Source*: http://en.wikipedia.org/w/index.php?title=File:Seal_of_Michigan.svg *License*: unknown *Contributors*: Designed by Lewis Cass

File:Map_of_USA_MI.svg *Source*: http://en.wikipedia.org/w/index.php?title=File:Map_of_USA_MI.svg *License*: Creative Commons Attribution 2.0 *Contributors*: Abnormaal, Hogweard, Huebi, Lokal Profil, Lupo, Mattbuck, Petr Dlouhý, 2 anonymous edits

File:Michigan 1718.jpg *Source*: http://en.wikipedia.org/w/index.php?title=File:Michigan_1718.jpg *License*: Public Domain *Contributors*: Original uploader was Billwhittaker at en.wikipedia

File:Hauling at Thomas Foster's, by Jenney, J A (detail).jpg *Source*: http://en.wikipedia.org/w/index.php?title=File:Hauling_at_Thomas_Foster's,_by_Jenney,_J_A_(detail).jpg *License*: unknown *Contributors*: Rmhermen

File:Granholm speaking to troops, Lansing, 1 Dec, 2005.jpg *Source*: http://en.wikipedia.org/w/index.php?title=File:Granholm_speaking_to_troops,_Lansing,_1_Dec,_2005.jpg *License*: Public Domain *Contributors*: SFC Jim Dowen, Jr.

File:Sleeping Bear Dune Aerial View.jpg *Source*: http://en.wikipedia.org/w/index.php?title=File:Sleeping_Bear_Dune_Aerial_View.jpg *License*: Public Domain *Contributors*: National Park Service employee

File:Tahquamenon falls upper.jpg *Source*: http://en.wikipedia.org/w/index.php?title=File:Tahquamenon_falls_upper.jpg *License*: Creative Commons Attribution 2.5 *Contributors*: User:anagy

File:Pointe Mouillee.jpg *Source*: http://en.wikipedia.org/w/index.php?title=File:Pointe_Mouillee.jpg *License*: Public Domain *Contributors*: U.S. Army Corps of Engineers, photographer not specified or unknown

File:Little Sable Light Point Light Station - Michigan.jpg *Source*: http://en.wikipedia.org/w/index.php?title=File:Little_Sable_Light_Point_Light_Station_-_Michigan.jpg *License*: Creative Commons Attribution 2.5 *Contributors*: Jjegers at en.wikipedia

File:Michigan.svg *Source*: http://en.wikipedia.org/w/index.php?title=File:Michigan.svg *License*: GNU Free Documentation License *Contributors*: Phizzy (talk).

File:MichiganHardinessZones.svg *Source*: http://en.wikipedia.org/w/index.php?title=File:MichiganHardinessZones.svg *License*: GNU Free Documentation License *Contributors*: Phizzy (talk).

File:Michigan population map.png *Source*: http://en.wikipedia.org/w/index.php?title=File:Michigan_population_map.png *License*: GNU Free Documentation License *Contributors*: Original uploader was JimIrwin at en.wikipedia

File:MichiganAncestry.svg *Source*: http://en.wikipedia.org/w/index.php?title=File:MichiganAncestry.svg *License*: GNU Free Documentation License *Contributors*: Phizzy (talk). Original uploader was Phizzy at en.wikipedia

File:Michigan Cherries, 2009 July.jpg *Source*: http://en.wikipedia.org/w/index.php?title=File:Michigan_Cherries,_2009_July.jpg *License*: Creative Commons Attribution 2.0 *Contributors*: Steven Depolo

File:Grand Hotel-Mackinac Island.jpg *Source*: http://en.wikipedia.org/w/index.php?title=File:Grand_Hotel-Mackinac_Island.jpg *License*: Attribution *Contributors*: David Ball

File:Mackinac Bridge Sunset.jpg *Source*: http://en.wikipedia.org/w/index.php?title=File:Mackinac_Bridge_Sunset.jpg *License*: Creative Commons Attribution 3.0 *Contributors*: User:Dehk

File:Michigan entrance sign.JPG *Source*: http://en.wikipedia.org/w/index.php?title=File:Michigan_entrance_sign.JPG *License*: Public Domain *Contributors*: User:Lovemykia

File:Grskyline2.jpg *Source*: http://en.wikipedia.org/w/index.php?title=File:Grskyline2.jpg *License*: Public Domain *Contributors*: User:Bhyse23

File:1 Lansing Pan.jpg *Source*: http://en.wikipedia.org/w/index.php?title=File:1_Lansing_Pan.jpg *License*: GNU Free Documentation License *Contributors*: User Criticalthinker on en.wikipedia

File:Flint skyline2.jpg *Source*: http://en.wikipedia.org/w/index.php?title=File:Flint_skyline2.jpg *License*: Public Domain *Contributors*: Xnatedawgx, Yassie

File:DownTownAA1 copy.jpg *Source*: http://en.wikipedia.org/w/index.php?title=File:DownTownAA1_copy.jpg *License*: Creative Commons Attribution 3.0 *Contributors*: Alan Piracha (Alanmi88)

File:MichiganCities.svg *Source*: http://en.wikipedia.org/w/index.php?title=File:MichiganCities.svg *License*: GNU Free Documentation License *Contributors*: Phizzy (talk).

File:Flag of Japan.svg *Source*: http://en.wikipedia.org/w/index.php?title=File:Flag_of_Japan.svg *License*: Public Domain *Contributors*: Various

File:Flag of the People's Republic of China.svg *Source*: http://en.wikipedia.org/w/index.php?title=File:Flag_of_the_People's_Republic_of_China.svg *License*: Public Domain *Contributors*: User:Denelson83, User:SKopp, User:Shizhao, User:Zscout370

Image:Soo Locks-Sault-Ste Marie.png *Source*: http://en.wikipedia.org/w/index.php?title=File:Soo_Locks-Sault-Ste_Marie.png *License*: Public Domain *Contributors*: AnRo0002, Appraiser, Feydey, Geofrog, Jkelly, Juiced lemon, Kimdime, Mattes, Mircea, Rmhermen, Xnatedawgx, Yassie, 5 anonymous edits

Image:Last glacial vegetation map.png *Source*: http://en.wikipedia.org/w/index.php?title=File:Last_glacial_vegetation_map.png *License*: unknown *Contributors*: Ciaurlec, DieBuche, Fabartus, G.enn, Innotata, JMCC1, Joey-das-WBF, Jrockley, MaxEnt, Mmcannis, Santosga, SchuminWeb, Slomox, 4 anonymous edits

Image:Michigan 1718.jpg *Source*: http://en.wikipedia.org/w/index.php?title=File:Michigan_1718.jpg *License*: Public Domain *Contributors*: Original uploader was Billwhittaker at en.wikipedia

Image:Treaty of Paris by Benjamin West 1783.jpg *Source*: http://en.wikipedia.org/w/index.php?title=File:Treaty_of_Paris_by_Benjamin_West_1783.jpg *License*: Public Domain *Contributors*: Bogdan, Clindberg, Daderot, Jkllee, Man vyi, Nonenmac, Shakko, The Red Hat of Pat Ferrick

Image:Flint Sit-Down Strike window.jpg *Source*: http://en.wikipedia.org/w/index.php?title=File:Flint_Sit-Down_Strike_window.jpg *License*: unknown *Contributors*: Sheldon Dick

Image:Gerald Ford.jpg *Source*: http://en.wikipedia.org/w/index.php?title=File:Gerald_Ford.jpg *License*: Public Domain *Contributors*: David Hume Kennerly, White House.

Image:Michigan.svg *Source*: http://en.wikipedia.org/w/index.php?title=File:Michigan.svg *License*: GNU Free Documentation License *Contributors*: Phizzy (talk).

Image Sources, Licenses and Contributors

Image:Sleeping Bear Dune Aerial View.jpg *Source*: http://en.wikipedia.org/w/index.php?title=File:Sleeping_Bear_Dune_Aerial_View.jpg *License*: Public Domain *Contributors*: National Park Service employee

Image:Pointe Mouillee.jpg *Source*: http://en.wikipedia.org/w/index.php?title=File:Pointe_Mouillee.jpg *License*: Public Domain *Contributors*: U.S. Army Corps of Engineers, photographer not specified or unknown

Image:Little Traverse Bay at sunset.jpg *Source*: http://en.wikipedia.org/w/index.php?title=File:Little_Traverse_Bay_at_sunset.jpg *License*: Creative Commons Attribution-Sharealike 2.5 *Contributors*: Angr, Bkonrad, Dbenbenn, Shinka, Urban, Werewombat, Xnatedawgx

Image:MichiganHardinessZones.svg *Source*: http://en.wikipedia.org/w/index.php?title=File:MichiganHardinessZones.svg *License*: GNU Free Documentation License *Contributors*: Phizzy (talk).

Image:Michigan Basin 2.jpg *Source*: http://en.wikipedia.org/w/index.php?title=File:Michigan_Basin_2.jpg *License*: Public Domain *Contributors*: Avenue, Claurec, Didiervberghe, Kablammo, Rémih

File:FullLakeOfTheClouds.JPG *Source*: http://en.wikipedia.org/w/index.php?title=File:FullLakeOfTheClouds.JPG *License*: Public Domain *Contributors*: Photo by Troy A. Heck

File:Grand Mere Beech.jpg *Source*: http://en.wikipedia.org/w/index.php?title=File:Grand_Mere_Beech.jpg *License*: Creative Commons Attribution-Sharealike 3.0 *Contributors*: w:User:IvanTortugaCody Hough

File:Holland State Park.jpg *Source*: http://en.wikipedia.org/w/index.php?title=File:Holland_State_Park.jpg *License*: Creative Commons Attribution 2.0 *Contributors*: Shirl

File:Silver Lake Dunes Michigan 2.jpg *Source*: http://en.wikipedia.org/w/index.php?title=File:Silver_Lake_Dunes_Michigan_2.jpg *License*: Public Domain *Contributors*: Dale Fisher, U.S. Army Corps of Engineers

File:Proud Lake Recreation Area.jpg *Source*: http://en.wikipedia.org/w/index.php?title=File:Proud_Lake_Recreation_Area.jpg *License*: Creative Commons Attribution 2.0 *Contributors*: Pat Williams from Commerce Twp, MI, USA

File:Canoes AuSableRiverMI.jpg *Source*: http://en.wikipedia.org/w/index.php?title=File:Canoes_AuSableRiverMI.jpg *License*: Public Domain *Contributors*: unknown

File:Wagner Falls.jpg *Source*: http://en.wikipedia.org/w/index.php?title=File:Wagner_Falls.jpg *License*: Creative Commons Attribution-Sharealike 3.0 *Contributors*: User:Two Hearted River

File:USA Michigan location map.svg *Source*: http://en.wikipedia.org/w/index.php?title=File:USA_Michigan_location_map.svg *License*: Creative Commons Attribution 3.0 *Contributors*: User:Alexrk2

File:purple pog.svg *Source*: http://en.wikipedia.org/w/index.php?title=File:Purple_pog.svg *License*: Public Domain *Contributors*: Andux, Antonsusi, Juiced lemon, STyx, TwoWings, 1 anonymous edits

File:red pog.svg *Source*: http://en.wikipedia.org/w/index.php?title=File:Red_pog.svg *License*: Public Domain *Contributors*: User:Andux

Image:BayViewPetoskyMI.jpg *Source*: http://en.wikipedia.org/w/index.php?title=File:BayViewPetoskyMI.jpg *License*: Public Domain *Contributors*: Brian Conway

Image:CalumetHecla.jpg *Source*: http://en.wikipedia.org/w/index.php?title=File:CalumetHecla.jpg *License*: Public Domain *Contributors*: Photographer not credited.

Image:SS City of Milwaukee.jpg *Source*: http://en.wikipedia.org/w/index.php?title=File:SS_City_of_Milwaukee.jpg *License*: Public Domain *Contributors*: Bill Herd

Image:Steamer Columbia - Detroit MI - 1905.jpg *Source*: http://en.wikipedia.org/w/index.php?title=File:Steamer_Columbia_-_Detroit_MI_-_1905.jpg *License*: Public Domain *Contributors*: Mtsmallwood, Werewombat, Yann, 1 anonymous edits

Image:Cranbrook Tower and Quadrangle.jpg *Source*: http://en.wikipedia.org/w/index.php?title=File:Cranbrook_Tower_and_Quadrangle.jpg *License*: Creative Commons Attribution-Sharealike 2.0 *Contributors*: Bradley Portnoy, User:Piranhaex at en.wikipedia

Image:Alden B Dow House Midland MI.jpg *Source*: http://en.wikipedia.org/w/index.php?title=File:Alden_B_Dow_House_Midland_MI.jpg *License*: Public Domain *Contributors*: Dow, Howell, & Gilmore

Image:Herbert H Dow House Midland MI.jpg *Source*: http://en.wikipedia.org/w/index.php?title=File:Herbert_H_Dow_House_Midland_MI.jpg *License*: Public Domain *Contributors*: Andrew Jameson

Image:DurantDortCarriageCoOfficeFlintMI.JPG *Source*: http://en.wikipedia.org/w/index.php?title=File:DurantDortCarriageCoOfficeFlintMI.JPG *License*: Creative Commons Attribution-Sharealike 3.0 *Contributors*: User:Andrew Jameson

Image:TheHenryFordMuseumClockToweratNight.jpg *Source*: http://en.wikipedia.org/w/index.php?title=File:TheHenryFordMuseumClockToweratNight.jpg *License*: Creative Commons Attribution 3.0 *Contributors*: User:Parkerdr

Image:HenryFordEstateSWSide.jpg *Source*: http://en.wikipedia.org/w/index.php?title=File:HenryFordEstateSWSide.jpg *License*: Creative Commons Attribution 3.0 *Contributors*: User:Parkerdr

Image:Fisher Building Detroit.jpg *Source*: http://en.wikipedia.org/w/index.php?title=File:Fisher_Building_Detroit.jpg *License*: GNU Free Documentation License *Contributors*: A Generous German

Image:River Rouge tool and die8b00276r.jpg *Source*: http://en.wikipedia.org/w/index.php?title=File:River_Rouge_tool_and_die8b00276r.jpg *License*: Public Domain *Contributors*: Alfred T. Palmer

Image:Fort Michilimackinac.jpg *Source*: http://en.wikipedia.org/w/index.php?title=File:Fort_Michilimackinac.jpg *License*: Public Domain *Contributors*: Galteglise at en.wikipedia

Image:Foxdetroitmarqueenightshot2.jpg *Source*: http://en.wikipedia.org/w/index.php?title=File:Foxdetroitmarqueenightshot2.jpg *License*: GNU Free Documentation License *Contributors*: Mikerussel

Image:General Motors building 089833pv.jpg *Source*: http://en.wikipedia.org/w/index.php?title=File:General_Motors_building_089833pv.jpg *License*: Public Domain *Contributors*: Historic American Buildings Survey

Image:MackinacIsland GrandHotel.jpg *Source*: http://en.wikipedia.org/w/index.php?title=File:MackinacIsland_GrandHotel.jpg *License*: Creative Commons Attribution-Sharealike 2.0 *Contributors*: Eli Duke from Seattle, United States

Image:Guardianinterior.jpg *Source*: http://en.wikipedia.org/w/index.php?title=File:Guardianinterior.jpg *License*: Public Domain *Contributors*: Original uploader was Funnyhat at en.wikipedia

Image:Ernest Hemmingway Cottage Walloon Lake MI.jpg *Source*: http://en.wikipedia.org/w/index.php?title=File:Ernest_Hemmingway_Cottage_Walloon_Lake_MI.jpg *License*: Public Domain *Contributors*: John Scott Mendinghall

Image:Highland Park Ford plant.jpg *Source*: http://en.wikipedia.org/w/index.php?title=File:Highland_Park_Ford_plant.jpg *License*: GNU Free Documentation License *Contributors*: Andrew Jameson (talk) at en.wikipedia

Image Sources, Licenses and Contributors

Image:Huron Lightship early career.jpg *Source*: http://en.wikipedia.org/w/index.php?title=File:Huron_Lightship_early_career.jpg *License*: unknown *Contributors*: United States Coast GuardOriginal uploader was Asher196 at en.wikipedia

Image:MackinacIsland Downtown.jpg *Source*: http://en.wikipedia.org/w/index.php?title=File:MackinacIsland_Downtown.jpg *License*: Creative Commons Attribution-Sharealike 2.0 *Contributors*: Michael Sprague from Asheville, North Carolina

Image:Marshall MI Abner Pratt House.jpg *Source*: http://en.wikipedia.org/w/index.php?title=File:Marshall_MI_Abner_Pratt_House.jpg *License*: Public Domain *Contributors*: Susan Collins

Image:Michigan state capitol.jpg *Source*: http://en.wikipedia.org/w/index.php?title=File:Michigan_state_capitol.jpg *License*: GNU Free Documentation License *Contributors*: Nikopoley

File:MilwaukeeClipperStarboardStern.jpg *Source*: http://en.wikipedia.org/w/index.php?title=File:MilwaukeeClipperStarboardStern.jpg *License*: Creative Commons Attribution-Sharealike 3.0 *Contributors*: User:Cgodfrey

Image:North Manitou Island Lifesaving Station - Michigan.png *Source*: http://en.wikipedia.org/w/index.php?title=File:North_Manitou_Island_Lifesaving_Station_-_Michigan.png *License*: Public Domain *Contributors*: National Park ServiceOriginal uploader was Mgreason at en.wikipedia

Image:Parke-Davis Research Laboratory Detroit MI.jpg *Source*: http://en.wikipedia.org/w/index.php?title=File:Parke-Davis_Research_Laboratory_Detroit_MI.jpg *License*: Creative Commons Attribution-Sharealike 3.0 *Contributors*: User:Andrew Jameson

Image:Pewabic Pottery 1991.jpg *Source*: http://en.wikipedia.org/w/index.php?title=File:Pewabic_Pottery_1991.jpg *License*: Public Domain *Contributors*: Jill S. Topolski

Image:QuincyMineNo2Shafthouse.jpg *Source*: http://en.wikipedia.org/w/index.php?title=File:QuincyMineNo2Shafthouse.jpg *License*: Public Domain *Contributors*: Keweenaw National Historic Park, Dan Johnson

Image:St Clair River Tunnel - Port Huron Michigan.jpg *Source*: http://en.wikipedia.org/w/index.php?title=File:St_Clair_River_Tunnel_-_Port_Huron_Michigan.jpg *License*: Public Domain *Contributors*: User:Werewombat

Image:St Ignace Mission 2009.jpg *Source*: http://en.wikipedia.org/w/index.php?title=File:St_Ignace_Mission_2009.jpg *License*: Creative Commons Attribution-Sharealike 3.0 *Contributors*: User:Andrew Jameson

Image:USS Silversides;0823601.jpg *Source*: http://en.wikipedia.org/w/index.php?title=File:USS_Silversides;0823601.jpg *License*: unknown *Contributors*: PMG, Werewombat, Wwoods

Image:Reo factory 1977.jpg *Source*: http://en.wikipedia.org/w/index.php?title=File:Reo_factory_1977.jpg *License*: unknown *Contributors*: Ralph J. Christian, National Park Service

Image:Steamer Ste Claire c 1915.jpg *Source*: http://en.wikipedia.org/w/index.php?title=File:Steamer_Ste_Claire_c_1915.jpg *License*: Public Domain *Contributors*: Andrew Jameson, Doncram, Msmallwood, Werewombat, Yann

File:HPIM4356.JPG *Source*: http://en.wikipedia.org/w/index.php?title=File:HPIM4356.JPG *License*: GNU Free Documentation License *Contributors*: User:Hsxeric

File:Red pog.svg *Source*: http://en.wikipedia.org/w/index.php?title=File:Red_pog.svg *License*: Public Domain *Contributors*: User:Andux

Image:Saginaw-Bay City-Saginaw Township North CSA.png *Source*: http://en.wikipedia.org/w/index.php?title=File:Saginaw-Bay_City-Saginaw_Township_North_CSA.png *License*: Public Domain *Contributors*: Nyttend, Spyder Monkey

Image:I-75.svg *Source*: http://en.wikipedia.org/w/index.php?title=File:I-75.svg *License*: unknown *Contributors*: Augiasstallputzer, Ltljltlj, SPUI, 1 anonymous edits

Image:I-675.svg *Source*: http://en.wikipedia.org/w/index.php?title=File:I-675.svg *License*: unknown *Contributors*: Ltljltlj, SPUI, 1 anonymous edits

Image:M-13.svg *Source*: http://en.wikipedia.org/w/index.php?title=File:M-13.svg *License*: Public Domain *Contributors*: User:IW4

Image:M-46.svg *Source*: http://en.wikipedia.org/w/index.php?title=File:M-46.svg *License*: Public Domain *Contributors*: User:IW4

Image:M-47.svg *Source*: http://en.wikipedia.org/w/index.php?title=File:M-47.svg *License*: Public Domain *Contributors*: User:IW4

Image:M-52.svg *Source*: http://en.wikipedia.org/w/index.php?title=File:M-52.svg *License*: Public Domain *Contributors*: User:IW4

Image:M-58.svg *Source*: http://en.wikipedia.org/w/index.php?title=File:M-58.svg *License*: Public Domain *Contributors*: User:IW4

Image:M-81.svg *Source*: http://en.wikipedia.org/w/index.php?title=File:M-81.svg *License*: Public Domain *Contributors*: User:IW4

Image:M-84.svg *Source*: http://en.wikipedia.org/w/index.php?title=File:M-84.svg *License*: Public Domain *Contributors*: User:IW4

Image:Former Castle Station post office- Saginaw Michigan.png *Source*: http://en.wikipedia.org/w/index.php?title=File:Former_Castle_Station_post_office-_Saginaw_Michigan.png *License*: unknown *Contributors*: James W. Gault III, CrazyElk at en.wikipedia

File:Flag of Mexico.svg *Source*: http://en.wikipedia.org/w/index.php?title=File:Flag_of_Mexico.svg *License*: Public Domain *Contributors*: User:AlexCovarrubias

File:Flag of Nigeria.svg *Source*: http://en.wikipedia.org/w/index.php?title=File:Flag_of_Nigeria.svg *License*: Public Domain *Contributors*: User:Jhs

File:Map of Michigan highlighting Saginaw County.svg *Source*: http://en.wikipedia.org/w/index.php?title=File:Map_of_Michigan_highlighting_Saginaw_County.svg *License*: Public Domain *Contributors*: User:Dbenbenn

File:Map of USA MI.svg *Source*: http://en.wikipedia.org/w/index.php?title=File:Map_of_USA_MI.svg *License*: Creative Commons Attribution 2.0 *Contributors*: Abnormaal, Hogweard, Huebi, Lokal Profil, Lupo, Mattbuck, Petr Dlouhý, 2 anonymous edits

Image:US 23.svg *Source*: http://en.wikipedia.org/w/index.php?title=File:US_23.svg *License*: Public Domain *Contributors*: Bidgee, Rocket000, SPUI, Xnatedawgx, 4 anonymous edits

Image:M-15.svg *Source*: http://en.wikipedia.org/w/index.php?title=File:M-15.svg *License*: Public Domain *Contributors*: User:IW4

Image:M-54.svg *Source*: http://en.wikipedia.org/w/index.php?title=File:M-54.svg *License*: Public Domain *Contributors*: User:IW4

Image:M-57.svg *Source*: http://en.wikipedia.org/w/index.php?title=File:M-57.svg *License*: Public Domain *Contributors*: User:IW4

Image:M-83.svg *Source*: http://en.wikipedia.org/w/index.php?title=File:M-83.svg *License*: Public Domain *Contributors*: User:IW4

File:Flag of the United States.svg *Source*: http://en.wikipedia.org/w/index.php?title=File:Flag_of_the_United_States.svg *License*: Public Domain *Contributors*: User:Dbenbenn, User:Indolences, User:Jacobolus, User:Technion, User:Zscout370

File:Flag of Michigan.svg *Source*: http://en.wikipedia.org/w/index.php?title=File:Flag_of_Michigan.svg *License*: unknown *Contributors*: Awg1010, Denelson83, Dzordzm, Fry1989, Homo lupus Mattes, Serinde, Svgalbertian, Werewombat, 1 anonymous edits

Image:I-69.svg *Source*: http://en.wikipedia.org/w/index.php?title=File:I-69.svg *License*: unknown *Contributors*: Augiasstallputzer, Ltljltlj, Rocket000, SPUI

Image Sources, Licenses and Contributors

Image:I-475.svg *Source*: http://en.wikipedia.org/w/index.php?title=File:I-475.svg *License*: unknown *Contributors*: Ltljltlj, SPUI

Image:US 10.svg *Source*: http://en.wikipedia.org/w/index.php?title=File:US_10.svg *License*: Public Domain *Contributors*: Rocket000, SPUI

Image:M-19.svg *Source*: http://en.wikipedia.org/w/index.php?title=File:M-19.svg *License*: Public Domain *Contributors*: User:IW4

Image:M-20.svg *Source*: http://en.wikipedia.org/w/index.php?title=File:M-20.svg *License*: Public Domain *Contributors*: User:IW4

Image:M-21.svg *Source*: http://en.wikipedia.org/w/index.php?title=File:M-21.svg *License*: Public Domain *Contributors*: User:IW4

Image:M-24.svg *Source*: http://en.wikipedia.org/w/index.php?title=File:M-24.svg *License*: Public Domain *Contributors*: User:IW4

Image:M-25.svg *Source*: http://en.wikipedia.org/w/index.php?title=File:M-25.svg *License*: Public Domain *Contributors*: User:IW4

Image:Business Loop 94.svg *Source*: http://en.wikipedia.org/w/index.php?title=File:Business_Loop_94.svg *License*: unknown *Contributors*: I-215, KelleyCook, Ltljltlj, Mountain169257, SPUI, T2, 1 anonymous edits

Image:M-29.svg *Source*: http://en.wikipedia.org/w/index.php?title=File:M-29.svg *License*: Public Domain *Contributors*: User:IW4

Image:M-30.svg *Source*: http://en.wikipedia.org/w/index.php?title=File:M-30.svg *License*: Public Domain *Contributors*: User:IW4

Image:M-53.svg *Source*: http://en.wikipedia.org/w/index.php?title=File:M-53.svg *License*: Public Domain *Contributors*: User:IW4

Image:M-90.svg *Source*: http://en.wikipedia.org/w/index.php?title=File:M-90.svg *License*: Public Domain *Contributors*: User:IW4

Image:M-136.svg *Source*: http://en.wikipedia.org/w/index.php?title=File:M-136.svg *License*: Public Domain *Contributors*: User:IW4

Image:M-138.svg *Source*: http://en.wikipedia.org/w/index.php?title=File:M-138.svg *License*: Public Domain *Contributors*: User:IW4

Image:M-142.svg *Source*: http://en.wikipedia.org/w/index.php?title=File:M-142.svg *License*: Public Domain *Contributors*: User:IW4

File:Blue Water Bridge (Port Huron Mich) Panorama.jpg *Source*: http://en.wikipedia.org/w/index.php?title=File:Blue_Water_Bridge_(Port_Huron_Mich)_Panorama.jpg *License*: Creative Commons Attribution-Sharealike 3.0 *Contributors*: Chris Light (talk) at en.wikipedia

File:Former Castle Station post office- Saginaw Michigan.png *Source*: http://en.wikipedia.org/w/index.php?title=File:Former_Castle_Station_post_office-_Saginaw_Michigan.png *License*: unknown *Contributors*: James W. Gault III, CrazyElk at en.wikipedia

File:Saginaw Trail map.svg *Source*: http://en.wikipedia.org/w/index.php?title=File:Saginaw_Trail_map.svg *License*: Public Domain *Contributors*: User:TwinsMetsFan

File:SaginawTrailCleaners 003.JPG *Source*: http://en.wikipedia.org/w/index.php?title=File:SaginawTrailCleaners_003.JPG *License*: Public Domain *Contributors*: TomCat4680 (talk)

Image:Tigers opening day2 2007.jpg *Source*: http://en.wikipedia.org/w/index.php?title=File:Tigers_opening_day2_2007.jpg *License*: unknown *Contributors*: User MJCdetroit on en.wikipedia

Image:Detroitfox3.jpg *Source*: http://en.wikipedia.org/w/index.php?title=File:Detroitfox3.jpg *License*: Creative Commons Attribution-Sharealike 2.5 *Contributors*: User:Mikerussell

File:WeatherballFlint.jpg *Source*: http://en.wikipedia.org/w/index.php?title=File:WeatherballFlint.jpg *License*: Public Domain *Contributors*: Original uploader was Steelbeard1 at en.wikipedia

File:M-10.svg *Source*: http://en.wikipedia.org/w/index.php?title=File:M-10.svg *License*: Public Domain *Contributors*: User:IW4

File:I-94.svg *Source*: http://en.wikipedia.org/w/index.php?title=File:I-94.svg *License*: unknown *Contributors*: Augiasstallputzer, Ltljltlj, SPUI, 1 anonymous edits

File:M-8.svg *Source*: http://en.wikipedia.org/w/index.php?title=File:M-8.svg *License*: Public Domain *Contributors*: User:IW4

File:M-102.svg *Source*: http://en.wikipedia.org/w/index.php?title=File:M-102.svg *License*: Public Domain *Contributors*: User:IW4

File:I-696.svg *Source*: http://en.wikipedia.org/w/index.php?title=File:I-696.svg *License*: unknown *Contributors*: Barack Obama Supporter, I-215, Kanonkas, KelleyCook, Ltljltlj, Mountain169257, Public Kanonkas 2, SPUI, 1 anonymous edits

Image:no image wide.svg *Source*: http://en.wikipedia.org/w/index.php?title=File:No_image_wide.svg *License*: Public Domain *Contributors*: SPUI, TwinsMetsFan

Image:Business plate.svg *Source*: http://en.wikipedia.org/w/index.php?title=File:Business_plate.svg *License*: unknown *Contributors*: Homefryes, Ltljltlj, RTCNCA, SPUI

File:Business Loop 75.svg *Source*: http://en.wikipedia.org/w/index.php?title=File:Business_Loop_75.svg *License*: unknown *Contributors*: Engleman, I-215, KelleyCook, Ltljltlj, Mountain169257, SPUI, T2, 1 anonymous edits

File:US 24.svg *Source*: http://en.wikipedia.org/w/index.php?title=File:US_24.svg *License*: Public Domain *Contributors*: Bidgee, SPUI, 2 anonymous edits

File:M-59.svg *Source*: http://en.wikipedia.org/w/index.php?title=File:M-59.svg *License*: Public Domain *Contributors*: User:IW4

File:M-15.svg *Source*: http://en.wikipedia.org/w/index.php?title=File:M-15.svg *License*: Public Domain *Contributors*: User:IW4

File:I-75.svg *Source*: http://en.wikipedia.org/w/index.php?title=File:I-75.svg *License*: unknown *Contributors*: Augiasstallputzer, Ltljltlj, SPUI, 1 anonymous edits

File:M-54.svg *Source*: http://en.wikipedia.org/w/index.php?title=File:M-54.svg *License*: Public Domain *Contributors*: User:IW4

File:I-69.svg *Source*: http://en.wikipedia.org/w/index.php?title=File:I-69.svg *License*: unknown *Contributors*: Augiasstallputzer, Ltljltlj, Rocket000, SPUI

File:M-21.svg *Source*: http://en.wikipedia.org/w/index.php?title=File:M-21.svg *License*: Public Domain *Contributors*: User:IW4

File:I-475.svg *Source*: http://en.wikipedia.org/w/index.php?title=File:I-475.svg *License*: unknown *Contributors*: Ltljltlj, SPUI

File:M-57.svg *Source*: http://en.wikipedia.org/w/index.php?title=File:M-57.svg *License*: Public Domain *Contributors*: User:IW4

File:M-83.svg *Source*: http://en.wikipedia.org/w/index.php?title=File:M-83.svg *License*: Public Domain *Contributors*: User:IW4

File:US 23.svg *Source*: http://en.wikipedia.org/w/index.php?title=File:US_23.svg *License*: Public Domain *Contributors*: Bidgee, Rocket000, SPUI, Xnatedawgx, 4 anonymous edits

File:M-46.svg *Source*: http://en.wikipedia.org/w/index.php?title=File:M-46.svg *License*: Public Domain *Contributors*: User:IW4

File:M-13.svg *Source*: http://en.wikipedia.org/w/index.php?title=File:M-13.svg *License*: Public Domain *Contributors*: User:IW4

Image:Saginawrivermap.png *Source*: http://en.wikipedia.org/w/index.php?title=File:Saginawrivermap.png *License*: Creative Commons Attribution-Sharealike 2.5 *Contributors*: User:Kmusser

file:Brucesky.jpg *Source*: http://en.wikipedia.org/w/index.php?title=File:Brucesky.jpg *License*: Public Domain *Contributors*: Brucegirl, P199, Themightyquill

Image Sources, Licenses and Contributors

file:Lake-Huron.svg *Source*: http://en.wikipedia.org/w/index.php?title=File:Lake-Huron.svg *License*: GNU Free Documentation License *Contributors*: Phizzy (talk). Original uploader was Phizzy at en.wikipedia

Image:Lake-huron-ipperwash-beach.jpg *Source*: http://en.wikipedia.org/w/index.php?title=File:Lake-huron-ipperwash-beach.jpg *License*: Creative Commons Attribution-Sharealike 2.5 *Contributors*: Original uploader was Msoccer29 at en.wikipedia

File:Lake Huron from Upper Peninsula.JPG *Source*: http://en.wikipedia.org/w/index.php?title=File:Lake_Huron_from_Upper_Peninsula.JPG *License*: Creative Commons Attribution-Sharealike 3.0 *Contributors*: User:NarparMI

Image:Lake Huron.jpg *Source*: http://en.wikipedia.org/w/index.php?title=File:Lake_Huron.jpg *License*: Creative Commons Attribution-Sharealike 2.5 *Contributors*: User:Hgjudd

Image:Dow-Event-Center-Saginaw-MI.jpg *Source*: http://en.wikipedia.org/w/index.php?title=File:Dow-Event-Center-Saginaw-MI.jpg *License*: Creative Commons Attribution 2.5 *Contributors*: Mrmiscellanious

File:Flag of the Czech Republic.svg *Source*: http://en.wikipedia.org/w/index.php?title=File:Flag_of_the_Czech_Republic.svg *License*: Public Domain *Contributors*: special commission (of code): SVG version by cs:-xfi-. Colors according to Appendix No. 3 of czech legal Act 3/1993. cs:Zirland.

File:Flag of Canada.svg *Source*: http://en.wikipedia.org/w/index.php?title=File:Flag_of_Canada.svg *License*: Public Domain *Contributors*: User:E Pluribus Anthony, User:Mzajac

File:Flag of Russia.svg *Source*: http://en.wikipedia.org/w/index.php?title=File:Flag_of_Russia.svg *License*: Public Domain *Contributors*: Zscout370

Image:PD-icon.svg *Source*: http://en.wikipedia.org/w/index.php?title=File:PD-icon.svg *License*: Public Domain *Contributors*: User:Duesentrieb, User:Rfl

File:Interstate 75 map.png *Source*: http://en.wikipedia.org/w/index.php?title=File:Interstate_75_map.png *License*: unknown *Contributors*: w:User:StratosphereNick Nolte

File:Florida 826.svg *Source*: http://en.wikipedia.org/w/index.php?title=File:Florida_826.svg *License*: Public Domain *Contributors*: SFUI

File:Toll Florida 924.svg *Source*: http://en.wikipedia.org/w/index.php?title=File:Toll_Florida_924.svg *License*: Public Domain *Contributors*: SPUI

File:I-4.svg *Source*: http://en.wikipedia.org/w/index.php?title=File:I-4.svg *License*: unknown *Contributors*: Augiasstallputzer, EugeneZelenko, Juliancolton, Kazuya35, Ltljltlj, Rocket000, SPUI, 1 anonymous edits

File:I-85.svg *Source*: http://en.wikipedia.org/w/index.php?title=File:I-85.svg *License*: unknown *Contributors*: Augiasstallputzer, Ltljltlj, SPUI, 2 anonymous edits

File:I-10.svg *Source*: http://en.wikipedia.org/w/index.php?title=File:I-10.svg *License*: unknown *Contributors*: Augiasstallputzer, Infrogmation, Juliancolton, Ltljltlj, Rocket000, SPUI, 1 anonymous edits

File:I-20.svg *Source*: http://en.wikipedia.org/w/index.php?title=File:I-20.svg *License*: unknown *Contributors*: Ltljltlj, SPUI, 2 anonymous edits

File:I-24.svg *Source*: http://en.wikipedia.org/w/index.php?title=File:I-24.svg *License*: unknown *Contributors*: Ltljltlj, SPUI, 1 anonymous edits

File:I-40.svg *Source*: http://en.wikipedia.org/w/index.php?title=File:I-40.svg *License*: unknown *Contributors*: Augiasstallputzer, Ltljltl, SPUI, Xnatedawgx, 1 anonymous edits

File:I-64.svg *Source*: http://en.wikipedia.org/w/index.php?title=File:I-64.svg *License*: unknown *Contributors*: Augiasstallputzer, Ltljltl, Rocket000, SPUI, Xnatedawgx

File:I-74.svg *Source*: http://en.wikipedia.org/w/index.php?title=File:I-74.svg *License*: unknown *Contributors*: Augiasstallputzer, Ltljltl, SPUI, Xnatedawgx, 1 anonymous edits

File:I-70.svg *Source*: http://en.wikipedia.org/w/index.php?title=File:I-70.svg *License*: Public Domain *Contributors*: , ,

File:I-80.svg *Source*: http://en.wikipedia.org/w/index.php?title=File:I-80.svg *License*: Public Domain *Contributors*: User:Ltljltlj

File:I-90.svg *Source*: http://en.wikipedia.org/w/index.php?title=File:I-90.svg *License*: unknown *Contributors*: Augiasstallputzer, Ltljltl, SPUI, 2 anonymous edits

File:OhioTurnpike.svg *Source*: http://en.wikipedia.org/w/index.php?title=File:OhioTurnpike.svg *License*: Public Domain *Contributors*: Ltljltlj, NE2, 1 anonymous edits

Image:Mackinac Bridge.jpg *Source*: http://en.wikipedia.org/w/index.php?title=File:Mackinac_Bridge.jpg *License*: Creative Commons Attribution-Sharealike 2.5 *Contributors*: Original uploader was Jeffness at en.wikipedia. Later version(s) were uploaded by Sam at en.wikipedia.

Image:Atlanta 75.85.jpg *Source*: http://en.wikipedia.org/w/index.php?title=File:Atlanta_75.85.jpg *License*: GNU Free Documentation License *Contributors*: Original uploader was Atlantacitizen at en.wikipedia

Image:I-blank.svg *Source*: http://en.wikipedia.org/w/index.php?title=File:I-blank.svg *License*: unknown *Contributors*: Augiasstallputzer, Ltljltlj, RTCNCA, SPUI, Sehome Bay, Sfan00 IMG, 2 anonymous edits

File:Florida 74.svg *Source*: http://en.wikipedia.org/w/index.php?title=File:Florida_74.svg *License*: Public Domain *Contributors*: SPUI

File:Florida 75.svg *Source*: http://en.wikipedia.org/w/index.php?title=File:Florida_75.svg *License*: Public Domain *Contributors*: SPUI

File:Georgia 74.svg *Source*: http://en.wikipedia.org/w/index.php?title=File:Georgia_74.svg *License*: Public Domain *Contributors*: User:Fredddie, User:Pedriana

File:Georgia 75.svg *Source*: http://en.wikipedia.org/w/index.php?title=File:Georgia_75.svg *License*: Public Domain *Contributors*: User:Fredddie, User:Pedriana

File:Elongated circle 74.svg *Source*: http://en.wikipedia.org/w/index.php?title=File:Elongated_circle_74.svg *License*: Public Domain *Contributors*: Northenglish

File:Elongated circle 75.svg *Source*: http://en.wikipedia.org/w/index.php?title=File:Elongated_circle_75.svg *License*: Public Domain *Contributors*: Northenglish

File:I-76.svg *Source*: http://en.wikipedia.org/w/index.php?title=File:I-76.svg *License*: unknown *Contributors*: Augiasstallputzer, Fran Rogers, Ltljltlj, SPUI, 1 anonymous edits

File:M-74.svg *Source*: http://en.wikipedia.org/w/index.php?title=File:M-74.svg *License*: Public Domain *Contributors*: User:IW4

File:M-75.svg *Source*: http://en.wikipedia.org/w/index.php?title=File:M-75.svg *License*: Public Domain *Contributors*: User:IW4

File:M-47.svg *Source*: http://en.wikipedia.org/w/index.php?title=File:M-47.svg *License*: Public Domain *Contributors*: User:IW4

File:Michigan 47 map.png *Source*: http://en.wikipedia.org/w/index.php?title=File:Michigan_47_map.png *License*: unknown *Contributors*: w:User:StratosphereNick Nolte

File:M-58.svg *Source*: http://en.wikipedia.org/w/index.php?title=File:M-58.svg *License*: Public Domain *Contributors*: User:IW4

File:US 10.svg *Source*: http://en.wikipedia.org/w/index.php?title=File:US_10.svg *License*: Public Domain *Contributors*: Rocket000, SPUI

File:M-48.svg *Source*: http://en.wikipedia.org/w/index.php?title=File:M-48.svg *License*: Public Domain *Contributors*: User:IW4

File:M-110.svg *Source*: http://en.wikipedia.org/w/index.php?title=File:M-110.svg *License*: Public Domain *Contributors*: User:IW4

Image:M-111 cutout.svg *Source*: http://en.wikipedia.org/w/index.php?title=File:M-111_cutout.svg *License*: Public Domain *Contributors*: User:Imzadi1979

Image Sources, Licenses and Contributors

File:US 112 Michigan 1926.svg *Source*: http://en.wikipedia.org/w/index.php?title=File:US_112_Michigan_1926.svg *License*: Public Domain *Contributors*: User:Scott5114

CPSIA information can be obtained
at www.ICGtesting.com
Printed in the USA
LVHW060929250122
709154LV00024B/960